A Wine Lover's Guide to Port

the Inside Story of a Unique Fortified Wine

ASSOCIAÇÃO DAS EMPRESAS DE VINHO DO PORTO

A Wine Lover's Guide to Port

the Inside Story of a Unique Fortified Wine

JOÃO PAULO MARTINS

PUBLICAÇÕES DOM QUIXOTE

Publicações Dom Quixote, Lda.
Rua Cintura do Porto
Urbanização da Matinha, Lote A – 2° C
1900-649 Lisboa • Portugal

This edition is sponsored by
Associação das Empresas de Vinho do Porto – AEVP
Rua Barão de Forrester, 412
4400-034 Vila Nova de Gaia . Portugal

English text by: Magdalena Gorrell Guimaraens

Cover by: Patrícia Proença

Graphic design and layout: Patrícia Proença
assisted by Susana Sá Santos

Photographs: **João Paulo Sottomayor**
pp. 6, 8, 15, 29, 39, 42, 43, 78-79, 82, 84, 86-87, 90, 92, 95, 100,
107, 110, 116, 118 – down, 124, 128, 129, 130 e 134;
Colecção do Instituto do Vinho do Porto
pp.10, 16-17, 20, 22, 24, 27, 30, 40, 45, 49, 50, 52, 54, 57, 59, 63, 64,
69, 70-down, 72, 73, 83, 93, 96,104,109,117,118-up, 121,
122, 127, 131, 137, 140, 141, 142;
Centro Português de Fotografia – Espólio do Fotógrafo Alvão
pp. 11, 48, 53, 66, 70-up, 75, 77, 94, 99, 120, 132, 135, 145, 146;
João Paulo Martins
pp. 34.

1st. edition: January 2001
Legal deposit n°: 156 322/00
Pre-press: Critério–Produção Gráfica
Printing and Binding: Printer Portuguesa

ISBN: 972-20-1781-0

Preface

This booklet on Port Wine is sponsored by the *AEVP* – Port Wine Shippers' Association which, from the very beginning, enthusiastically encouraged me and gave me a totally free hand to organise my material, choose the topics and attribute to each the importance I alone felt was most appropriate.

At all times, the *Port Wine Institute* was always willing and available to answer my questions and give me the information, data and many of the photographs I have used as illustrations.

The *Casa do Douro* supplied me with all the information I needed on the registry of Douro vineyards, as well as much additional published material.

I knocked on many Port Wine doors in order to clear up doubts, ask for information and confirm data and I was always received with great interest and a total willingness to assist me in my research.

The *Centro Português de Fotografia* in Porto that houses the complete collection of this famous photographer's work kindly supplied several of the Alvão photographs. Considering that this collection numbers more than 120,000 photos that are only now beginning to be catalogued, this would have been an almost impossible task had it not been for the help I obtained from the Centro staff who also told me that several photos I had chosen had never before been published. There must be many, many more.

Lastly, a special word of thanks to João Paulo Sotto Mayor who graciously offered me my choice of photographs from his collection on the Douro and Port Wine.

Douro landscape.

Introduction

*T*he booklet that you are holding is a Handbook on Port Wine. With it, I hope to help consumers acquire a better understanding and appreciation for Port. This is not a scientific treatise, nor is it the culmination of years of academic research. Although I consulted the principle technical literature of today, both in Portuguese, French and mainly, English, my purpose was not to fill these pages with scholarly pronouncements. This is why I have omitted footnotes and endnotes, as well as a list of bibliographic references. This is essentially the work of a journalist who has combined the information he obtained from the literature with his personal knowledge of the Douro, of the shippers in Vila Nova de Gaia and of the wines – a journalist whose profession has offered him the opportunity to taste several hundreds of different Ports from practically every single house in the trade.

There is no end to the amount of information on Port that is available. As a result of Port's long-standing links to the British market, for over a century the British have quite naturally dedicated themselves to studying this wine. Anyone who is seriously interested in learning more about Port cannot avoid consulting the immense number of documents in English – profound scientific and academic papers, passionate personal outpourings and/or political pamphlets.

There is also a considerable amount of literature in Portuguese: in addition to 200 years' worth of legislation on this matter, there is a wealth of commercial documents to be found in company files and in Customs and Excise records and a wide range of other papers, from provocative political pamphlets flavoured with the Liberal spirit of the 19th century to in depth studies that indelibly marked the understanding of the region.

There remains, however, much to be done. The work of researchers would be greatly assisted if someone were to make a methodical study of the wealth of documents and assorted papers that are stored at the Port firms. Moreover, there still is a certain amount of material of dubious credibility that needs to be examined and confirmed.

The first steps to such research have been taken there has been renewed interest in the Douro and the history of Port Wine in very recent years. In Vila Real, a group of historians from the University of Trás-os-Montes created the *GEHVID* (a group dedicated to studying the history of Douro viticulture and Port Wine); this entity has been particularly active and has published many papers on Port, mainly in the journal *Revista Douro – Estudos e Documentos*. Many foreign researchers are actively "diving" into archives and presenting exciting new theories on subjects that had, heretofore, been tacitly accepted. History now is being examined in the light of the anthropology, sociology, demography and economics of the region. If occasionally the field of observation is almost minimal and highly localised, as in the case of individual case studies, there is no doubt that there is a sufficient abundance of subjects involving Port to attract numerous more researchers.

Loading pipes of Port.

Porto at the turn of the 19th century.

From a more practical aspect there is the work of *ADVID* – Association for the Development of Douro Viticulture, founded in 1980 by several companies in the sector with a view to encouraging field studies on viticulture and rendering technical assistance to farmers. Much of its scientific work has already been published and we are expecting a great deal in the future from this Association whose dynamism has proven to be of vital importance to the Douro.

As I wrote this booklet, uppermost in my mind was the need to ensure that the reader and the consumer should obtain the utmost pleasure when savouring this unique beverage, no matter how meaningful it would be to offer them an under-standing of all the aspects surrounding Port. Consequently, I did my best to describe the different types of Port, the meth-ods by which they are made and when it is best to drink them.

As regards Port's 300 year-old history, my intent was not to write a history book as this would have been beyond the scope of this work. The few historical references serve solely as background information to guide the reader.

Rabelo boats in Gaia.

1. The River, the City, the Wine

The *Ribeira* is one of the most typical districts in the City of Porto. Lying alongside the river that has so frequently betrayed the trust of those who live there by invading their homes and their shops, the Ribeira is a continuously bubbling caldron of life. Although in past times it was notorious for the immense activity generated by a never-ending stream of inward and outward-bound ships, today it is calmer but still busy as it bustles with tradesmen and women noisily hawking their wares, neighbourhood children flocking to the cool waters on hot summer days and tourists attempting to delve into its deepest secrets.

I suggest that you join me on a trip upriver to Pinhão on one of the many pleasure boats that sail the River Douro. The journey will enable us to see just how docile the river has become, as opposed to its violence of the past, as we travel up the several dams that were built to regulate and master the fury of the flow. It is hard to believe that there is nary a year when the river does not burst its banks to flood riverside villages and towns, with special impact downstream on the Ribeira in Porto and the quayside in Vila Nova de Gaia, the marks of which never cease to astound visitors to the Gaia wine lodges. In spite of its apparent domestication, the soul of the Douro remains unfettered, a constant reminder that the river still sets the pace for all those who venture within its realm.

The river may have fashioned the landscape but it was men who, over three centuries, built and re-built the hillsides rising from its banks. Men who discovered that the Douro was harbouring the potential for a fabulous wine handed down to us today under the name of Port. Men who discovered that all the good things that the Douro had to offer could only be obtained as a result of insanely difficult, exhausting work.

As we travel upriver the landscape changes – sometimes lush and green, other times dry; its valleys, sometimes shallow, other times deep set; steep, rugged hillsides sculptured by the hands of men who unearthed the secrets of transforming a terrain better suited to unrestrained scrub and wild animals into fertile terraces.

This is the land where Port was born between fragments of broken slabs of schistous rock, so important to the quality of the wine; a land of scorching hot summers and bone-chilling cold winters; a land of great extremes and excesses.

The same landscape greets us along the valleys of the rivers that flow into the River Douro, where vineyards are the almost sole agricultural activity in the region. Wine rules here. Here, the year begins and ends as a function of the vintage, the harvesting of the grapes; here, wine determines the pace of the day-to-day routine.

Soon after its birth, the wine travels down river to rest in the cool, dark wine lodges of Vila Nova de Gaia, across the river from Porto. Throughout its history, Port has been the product of the marriage between the Douro where it is born and the City of Porto - actually, Vila Nova de Gaia - where it grows and matures and from whence it was once embarked on the ships that swarmed alongside the quays of Porto and Gaia, by the thousands of pipes each year.

The entire history of this wine is marked by Man's labour. Although greatly eased by the introduction of new technologies, the work of men remains indispensable to the production of the wide range of wines from the Douro region. Workers from far-off lands contributed to creating the Douro that we know today – Galicians from Northern Spain who, in their thousands, built the pre-phylloxera terraces; the *rogas*, groups of itinerant workers from neighbouring villages and hamlets, who came and still come at the time of the vintage to pick the grapes and without whom the grapes could not be trod.

Now that we have finished our trip to the Douro region, let's return by train and visit the place to which the wine is sent on the second stage of its journey to the consumer. In Vila Nova de Gaia, thousands of casks of wine are carefully stored in dozens of wine lodges where time appears to being standing still. Here there is no hustle and bustle, there is no scorching summer heat, no bone-chilling winter cold. Silence is golden. It is here, amidst pipes stacked one upon another on hard-packed earth floors, under dark tiled roofs, that we find the miracle of turning Douro wine into Port. Douro wine, a harsh and difficult product, transformed by the art of Man into a sweet, soft, light nectar bursting with rich and incomparably delicate aromas.

In the very beginning, Port was mostly drunk by the elite in society. From its origins as an aristocratic wine first consumed

primarily by the British, it is now a beverage that can be savoured by all those who are looking for a unique wine. At one time, Port containing very small doses of quinine – the so-called *Porto Quinado* was a very popular aperitif in very hot climates such as Africa where people believed that it also helped to protect them from malaria.

The aristocratic nature of this wine has not entirely disappeared. Not only does it continue to be the most noble of beverages at very exclusive private London Clubs as, not surprisingly so, it is honoured with considerable decorum in Porto at the Factory House, the equally exclusive *Clube*

Pipes' transport in Douro.

Portuense and on the occasion of Port Wine Brotherhood ceremonies.

At this turn of the century, Port continues to be discovered by new consumers and although most is still sold in Europe, it is highly significant that new markets such as the USA are becoming increasingly interested in Port. It is quite likely that Port is still far from reaching the acme of its splendid career. There are still more consumers to attract, more of the Douro region to explore, much more left to study and to discover. Such is the fascination that lures and binds those who work in the Douro.

2. The Pleasure of Port

Port is a wine with multiple characteristics. It can be consumed on numerous occasions. In fact, Port lovers usually say that the best time to drink Port is... when you feel like it! The prevailing idea is that Port requires no special excuse, no special occasion, and no special accompaniment to be savoured with pleasure.

Port Wine is a world of its own. History took care to create several different types of Port; the wine lover who wishes to make the most of this unique wine needs to understand the different types that are offered to him. Only thus will he be able to obtain the maximum pleasure from each type and adapt each wine to the right moment and to the most appropriate accompaniment.

There are several ways by which the various types of Port may be classified, one being by colour: Port is either white or red. So far, the same as other wines. However, although the most famous Ports are, without a shadow of a doubt, the red Ports, White Port has a long and noble history that deserves some additional information.

WHITE PORT

The family of White Port is composed of two very different types of wine: young white Ports that are sold soon after they are made and are mainly drunk as aperitifs; and old white Ports that have aged in wood, are more oxidised and, like the tawnies, are drunk after meals. There is an enormous difference in style between these two classes of White Port, their aromas are very different and their quality is not a point of comparison. Old White Ports are usually expensive wines

Shades of White Port - from the young (on the left) to the old (on the right).

sold in limited quantities by shippers, more as a prestige product rather than as a wine destined to be sold in large amounts and with a great turnover.

It is very difficult for the less expert consumer to distinguish between a very old white and an equally old tawny. The fact of the matter is that time has brought them closer together: with age, tawnies lose their purple red colour and gradually acquire a reddish-brown tone. Whites do the same: with age and as they oxidise in wood, they become the colour of old gold so that at the end of 15 or 20 years there is little difference in colour between them. When both are of excellent quality, a superior Old White Port is equally as fine as an Old Tawny Port.

You must not think, however, that there is an abundance of old White Port on the market. Very few Port houses still ship this kind of wine. If you are lucky enough to find a wine such as the one I just described, the pleasure that you will obtain from drinking it will more than justify the high price you will have to pay. What you will usually find on the market are White Ports that should be drunk when young and which do not justify a lengthy description. A Young

White Port is an aperitif wine, one that can be served with a slice of lemon, with tonic water, ice and lemon, or just chilled. This is a perfect drink for a hot summer's day; a beverage that goes down smoothly; an uncomplicated wine, with little history.

Furthermore, within the family of White Port, there are several types of wine from which to choose according to their degree of sweetness, ranging from the extra dry to the sweet – also known as *Lágrima*. All these wines have a degree of alcohol similar to red Port (between 19° and 22°), except for Light Dry White where the alcohol content is only 16.5°.

When you choose a White Port you must mainly think of when and how you plan to serve it. You must bear in mind that young whites whose colour is very similar to other, non-fortified, wines usually have less aroma than an ordinary dry white wine to which no grape spirit has been added, because adding brandy tends to destroy most of the more subtle and volatile aromas in the wine. This is one reason why White Port has less of a bouquet and is best drunk with the "help" of a slice of lemon, a splash of tonic or some other mixer.

Although White Port is very popular in some countries, it is almost unknown in others. Portugal is one of the markets that consumes a lot of White Port and this wine is becoming increasingly popular in France. More traditional markets such as the British market continue to prefer Red Port, the king of Port.

RED PORT

The overwhelming majority of Port that is sold is made from red grapes. Today, white and red grapes are separated when they arrive at the winery, but this was not always so. Traditionally, in the Douro, white and red grapevines were planted side by side in the vineyards and you would often see different varieties of both white and red growing together. Naturally, the wine that was made would include a goodly amount of white grapes.

There are few old vineyards today where the vines continue to be mixed as producers prefer to organise the planting of their vineyards according to varietal as it enables them to pick the grapes when each type has reached its ideal moment of maturation. A traditional Douro practice has disappeared but the result is frankly better. The must that is produced today is much better balanced and the winemaker can more easily determine the future destination of each lot of wine he makes.

The red grapes that go into making Port present a wide range of characteristics. Some produce more concentrated musts, others are preferred because of their abundant production, some are very aromatic but not very acid, and so on. The winemaker must therefore decide what he is going to do with each type of wine.

The first step he needs to do is to decide, according to the quality of the wine, whether it has a structure and is of a quality that would enable it to age for long periods in wood. In this event, the wine is transferred to casks (usually containing between 600 and 640 litres) or to medium-sized or very large vats (*tonéis* and *balseiros*). The purpose of storing the wine for long periods in wood is not for it to acquire the aroma of the wood (contrary to that which is practised for table wine), but rather to allow the wine to develop through oxidation in casks and vats made from old, wine-seasoned wood.

With time, Tawny Port loses colour.

Another initial decision of great importance is to determine whether the wine will be sold as a young wine or not and as a Ruby, Vintage Character, LBV or Vintage Port. In all these cases, the winemaker will want to retain the red colour of the wine and its young, fruity aromas. These wines are not kept in small casks but in very large vats to ensure a minimum of oxidation and the characteristics of a young wine. They will be bottled young and some of them – Vintage or LBV – will then proceed to age in bottle.

PORT – AGED IN WOOD OR IN BOTTLE?

Thus, the winemaker has intentionally created two distinctly separate Port families: Ports that age in wood and those that age in bottle. Neither of these has much in common with the other, other than the fact that both are Port and both are usually of a superior quality.

This organisation of Port into two completely different groups results from the evolution of Port throughout its history as the styles that we know today did not exist at the very beginning of the 18th century. Indeed, in Port's very early infancy, little importance or commercial value was attributed to old wine that had aged for long periods in wood. In those days and throughout the 19th century, consumers were much more interested in young wines, those that today are known as "Vintage" or earlier, by their old name, "*Novidade*".

I have the impression that even today, few shippers are interested in marketing very old wines. Business today revolves mainly around two different premises: better profits are obtained with current wines and greater prestige ensues from Vintage. The rest, is of secondary importance. If we look carefully at the price at which most houses sell a 10 Years Old tawny and then consider the investment in casks, in the space they occupy in the lodge, in the accumulated evaporation over ten years and the financial cost of this lengthy ageing process, the price normally charged for such a wine far from covers the expense of producing it. Today, any good

Port lodges in Vila Nova de Gaia.

Douro table wine has acquired a prestige that enables its producer to sell it for double the price of a 10 Years Old Tawny Port. If Port houses continue to sell these wines today, it is not for the profits they represent but because it is one of the traditional categories that have become well known to the consumer. Every Port house has its 10 Years Old Tawny, even if one could argue that this is not good business.

Several firms today are concentrating on certain types of wine that have become the flagship of their brand. Some have chosen Vintage Character and others are focusing on LBV that is more easily sold. It would appear that there is a trend in the Port trade for firms to stress the value of categories of Port that require a lower capital investment but still enable them to offer good quality wines at a more attractive price to the consumer.

Undoubtedly, old wines will continue to have a share of the market, although these wines, particularly the 20, 30 and Over 40 Years Old, are produced in very limited amounts. It is not unusual to hear a Port shipper say that he only bottles one or two pipes of 30 Years Old each year. This limited production is a guarantee of quality for the consumer as no shipper will risk his good name... for a couple of pipes of wine. These wines are so carefully cared for, so "coddled" and their quality is so protected, that the final result is always a very superior Port that the consumer can purchase with full confidence. Even in this class, there are different styles of wines but these are characteristics that unite rather than divide them. They are always expensive but their price is more than justified by their quality and the pleasure they offer those who drink them.

All Tawny Port is aged in wood. The designation tawny refers to the typical colour of a wine that has aged in wood: as the wine oxidises, the original purple red colour slowly becomes a golden reddish brown and the wine acquires certain characteristic aromas. In addition to this generic characteristic, there is a wide range of qualities in the family of Tawny Port.

First of all, to refine our description, Red Ports are divided into two groups: **Undated Ports** and **Dated Ports**.

UNDATED PORT WINE

Ruby

Ruby Port is exactly that: a red wine with the colour of the precious stone of the same name. In order for these wines to retain their bright red colour and the characteristics of a young wine, they are kept in very large vats that may contain several thousands of litres of wine, and practically never aired, instead of being stored in small casks and frequently transferred from one cask to another to encourage oxidation.

Ruby Port is a wine that must be drunk young, that remains fresh in the mouth and which is much to the taste of a great many consumers. Sold with an average age of 3 years, this is a red Port that does not improve in bottle and therefore should be drunk soon after it is purchased. Contrary to Tawny Port and because it has undergone a minimal oxidation, this wine will suffer from prolonged exposure to air which is why it should also be drunk as soon as possible after the bottle has been uncorked.

If I were to be forced to choose between a current Tawny and a young Ruby, I would undoubtedly pick the Ruby. This wine has been handled less, its flavour is closer to that of the original fruit, and it is more lively and true. Always a delightful drunk, it gives excellent value for the price.

Vintage Character

Within the class of Ruby Port there is another, superior category: Vintage Character. The name given to these wines is highly controversial and has led to considerable discussion within the Port trade. Many shippers do not agree with the use of the word "Vintage" as they believe that this designation could mislead the consumer. I agree. The word Vintage should be applied solely and exclusively to wines that are truly Vintage quality wines. This latter position is also highly controversial and shippers have yet to come to a consensus of opinions.

A Vintage Character Port is a better quality Ruby and it is precisely because of this that some firms have named these wines Reserve Ruby.

Vintage Character is more full-bodied and more concentrated than a standard Ruby; in other words, it must possess the "character of a Vintage". More and more consumers are becoming interested in these wines and with reason. When a consumer looks for a Port that reminds him of a Vintage he may not wish to pay the very high price he will be asked. A Vintage Character is an excellent choice.

Of all the wines in the medium price range, this is the category with the overall highest average quality. The fact itself that these wines are handled little, rarely aired or pumped from cask to cask, makes it possible for a shipper to offer a good quality, young wine.

Vintage Character does not mature well in bottle, as this wine is usually filtered before it is bottled which removes some of the components that would otherwise enable it to

Casks and vats in Gaia.

do so. To enjoy the full vigour of its youth, you should drink this wine when it is as young as possible.

In this category, also, you may come across situations that are somewhat confusing as not all wines that belong to the category of Vintage Character Port indicate this on the label. In such cases, the consumer does not know whether he is purchasing a standard Ruby or a Vintage Character. Although both belong to the same range of wines, their quality and price are different. I would therefore suggest that before you buy one of these wines you inform yourself beforehand or that you follow the advice of the shop's wine specialist.

Tawny

"Tawny" means golden reddish-brown. This is a wine that has aged in wood. When accompanied by no other des-ignation, Tawny Port corresponds to a standard wine.

Standard tawnies are the bottom of the range and they usually are an average of three years old. You will find a bit of everything here although there has been an improvement in the average quality of these wines as the introduction of new winemaking techniques, new wineries and new vineyards have began to bear fruit. The consumer should not, however, expect to find a highly unusual Port within this range. These are wines that are easily drunk, that are not really worth laying down and should be stored upright. Once open, a bottle may be drunk over one or two months. Here, too, there are a great many differences in style and quality from firm to firm.

Within the general group of tawnies there is also the **Reserve Tawny Port**, normally sold at between five and seven years of age. It is not always easy for the consumer to distinguish clearly between these Reserve tawnies as the language that appears on the labels varies considerably and differences are not always apparent.

In terms of colour, Reserve tawnies usually represent the midpoint between the characteristic red of a Ruby and the golden reddish-brown tones of a Tawny. Here, too, there are great differences in quality and you begin to see the distinctive house styles of the various shippers. By this I mean that these wines may vary considerably. Some are very deep in colour and others are reminiscent of older, more golden brown tawnies. Current legislation permits this diversity, thus respecting each firm's preferences.

It is up to the Port Wine Institute's Panel of Tasters to approve these wines and to certify their age (usually an average 7 years). Not all shippers make every single category of Port and there are some who do not even make a tawny of this type. Many consider this category to represent a transition (neither a young nor a 10 Years Old Tawny Port), with all the lack of definition that this implies: neither young nor old, it is hard to define exactly what this Reserve Tawny should be. According to its age, it should always be quite fruity as a sign of its youth and reveal some hint of dried fruit on the nose. It is also a wine that is easily drunk at the end of a meal. It does not improve in bottle and should be purchased as required and drunk immediately afterwards. Likewise, it should be stored upright, not on its side as you would with a table wine, as it does not have the same characteristics. It is the rule to lay table wines on their side so that the cork remains damp, thus preventing any air from entering the bottle and the oxidation of the wine. This is one reason why standard corks are rarely used for tawnies in favour of stoppers or corks that can be removed without a corkscrew. Furthermore, as this wine is subject to some oxidation before it is bottled, it can be drunk some time after the bottle has been uncorked, without its losing any quality.

Tawnies with an Indication of Age

This is the group of wines whose labels indicate the average age of the Port within the bottle: 10, 20, 30 Years Old or More than 40 Years Old. All these wines belong to the family of Tawny Port, that is, they are wines that have aged in wood through oxidation.

The indication of age is a sign that there are several different styles to these wines, according to each shipper. The fact is that current legislation does not stipulate that all the wine in the lot must necessarily be 10 years old, for example. What usually occurs is that the winemaker blends sev-

Port Wine must age slowly.

The many flavours of Tawny Port.

eral wines with different ages to form a lot whose average age is the one indicated on the label. In the case of the example of the 10 Years Old, some wine in the blend will be older and some will be younger. The difference in style that I mentioned earlier exists inasmuch as a firm's winemaker and taster, in order to remain faithful to a house style, will make a blend whose characteristics will remain essentially unchanged year after year. Thus, if one firm chooses to blend wines of different ages and another only selects wines that are 10 years old, or close to that age, the result will be vastly different.

The colour of a 10 year old Port is usually a transition between red and golden reddish brown, the latter being more characteristic of an oxidised wine.

In terms of market prices, ten-year-old Ports are grossly undervalued. They are sold far too cheaply for the quality that is required of a wine of this age. Regrettably, this difference between the cost and the selling price has led some operators in the sector to be less demanding as regards their standards than they would be, for example, for a twenty-year-old wine.

The small world of 10 year old Tawny Port has recently undergone some changes. After the entry into the market of producers-bottlers (1986), a few decided to sell wines with a 10 Years Old indication of age. In my experience, these wines have an average age greater than 10 years and their style is much more similar to that of 20 year old tawnies. These wines are always more full-bodied, much more brown and more oxidised, fruit of their ageing in the Douro region where scorching hot summer temperatures favour and accelerate the ageing process, thus making them somewhat baked in nature. I'm not going to speak of numbers as these wines are sold in minute quantities. Still, they have a certain style of their own that adds to the options offered to the consumer and their price is usually most attractive.

As we advance towards to the older Ports – 20, 30 and More than 40 Years Old – we find less and less available wine on the market. Not only are stocks very limited but the extremely high prices they fetch tend to discourage some consumers. Beyond 30 years old we are speaking of only a few pipes per year (per shipper) and there are even some firms who do not market a Port that is over 20 years old.

As to the price, it is not surprisingly high considering the great capital investment that goes into these wines, the annual loss of wine through evaporation and the great care that must be taken with them. These are prestige, not commercial, wines.

It is here, as we speak of Tawnies with an Indication of Age, that the art of blending comes truly into is own, the art of mixing different wines to obtain a result that is consistently faithful to a particular style, over and over again. This is not a case of bottling that which Nature produced, as with a Vintage Port; it is the oenologist's ability to build on, shape and perfect that which he is given to work with. This is a highly complex art that begins with the winemaker's skill in selecting very young wines that will be destined for ageing. He must have the expertise to identify the right aromas in the young wines and have a clear idea in his mind as to how they will develop as the wine ages in wood. It is daunting for the person who first comes to the world of Port Wine as he studies and gets to know the house style, a style that has been perfected through decades of work.

The oenologist's task becomes considerably easier when he is given a wide range of very different, quality wines to work with. In other words, it is much easier for a great house, with large stocks of wines of different ages, to make a lot of 20 Years Old Port than it is for a small producer who only has a few pipes of old wine in his cellar. An old wine usually needs to be blended with a younger wine to refresh it, to give it some youth and to ensure the total pleasure of he who drinks it.

As these wines do not improve in bottle, they should be drunk as they are purchased. They should be kept upright as there is no danger of an undesirable oxidation as by their very nature, they have already oxidised. Furthermore, as all these wines are filtered before they are bottled, they will not throw a deposit in bottle and therefore do not need to be decanted.

The date on which the wine was bottled must be indicated on either the front or back label. Therefore, I suggest that you look for the most recent date of bottling when you purchase such a wine.

Crusted

Crusted Port is a type of wine that few firms in the trade have paid much attention to. This is a Port made from blended wine from several years (usually two or three), aged for a minimum of two years in wood and then in bottle for three years before it is sold. As the wine is not filtered before bottling, it is likely to throw a deposit, that is, form a crust on the bottom of the bottle. The date on which it is bottled must be indicated on the label.

DATED PORTS

The wines that are included in this group – *Colheita, Garrafeira,* Late Bottled Vintage (LBV) and Vintage – represent only a small part of the Port shippers' business yet it is on them that a firm's prestige depends. No matter how much Port a firm sells, if its wines from the above categories are of average or less than average quality, it will never make the list of Great Port Houses. This explains why even more care is taken in selecting the wines for these categories.

These wines share the distinction that they are all wines from a single year which must be indicated on the label. In other words, from the moment they are made until they are bottled, these wines have not been blended or mixed with wine from a different year. There are several types.

Colheita

This is a Tawny Port, aged in wood and a minimum seven years old before it is bottled, although it may be sold older, if the producer so wishes it. This wine is usually only bottled as required by the market.

In some cases it is difficult to distinguish between a Colheita and a 10 Years Old Tawny Port. A Colheita is usually a superior quality wine although styles vary considerable from firm to firm. As with all other tawnies, it should be drunk at the end of a meal, slightly chilled. As this wine is filtered before it is bottled, it requires no decanting.

This wine may present a very interesting evolution in bottle. Although one cannot properly speak of an evolution in its structure, over the years it may acquire some aromas that are hard to define, usually referred to as a "bottle nose". These aromas result from the wine's having spent many years in contact with the glass of the bottle; consequently, Colheita Port tends to be crisper, almost austere, and present a most attractive delicacy.

This type of Port is very popular on the Portuguese market where it is often given as a birthday present, matching the year on the label with the lucky recipient's year of birth. You must not be surprised to find many different brands of wine for a same Colheita year. Sometimes, as in the case of Colheita 1937, several shippers purchased many pipes of Port made that year from the Casa do Douro. Even in the case of such elderly wines as this '37, you need not worry about the quality of the wine. The example of the Colheita 1937 is a perfect example: the wine is of excellent quality and many, many years will have to pass before it loses its aromatic richness and its nature as a wine to be drunk late in the evening.

Garrafeira – a novel concept

Only one Port house trades in Garrafeira Port – Niepoort. This is essentially a Tawny Port that is aged in wood for seven years before it is bottled in glass demijohns where it continues to age for several years.

Garrafeira wines ageing in wood – Niepoort lodges.

The unique nature of this wine arises from the fact that the Niepoort demijohns are authentic museum pieces – manufactured in Germany in the 18th century, they have a very unusual shape, contain approximately ten litres of wine each and produce a wine of bewildering characteristics. The colour is usually a deeper red than you would see in wines that have aged a long time in wood; on the nose, they strike a very original balance between some aromas of fruit and jam and the characteristic hint of dry fruit you would expect to find in a Tawny Port. Their many years in bottle give them the famous bottle nose that gives such crispness to wine. Difficult to categorise, you can however say that they fit in somewhere between an Old Tawny and an LBV that has remained many years in bottle.

These rare and very expensive wines are unique in the Port trade. Interestingly enough, you might wonder why Niepoort is the only firm that produces them. In my opinion, they are endowed with sufficient personality to justify a greater interest on the part of other shippers; apparently not. Their originality lies in the fact that there is no tradition in the trade for this type of wine; this is a tradition created by Niepoort who is wagering on continuing to trade in this oddity

Under the new law, the descriptor "Garrafeira" is permitted as long as it is used in association with Colheita.

Late Bottled Vintage (LBV)

This is also wine produced in a single year, black purple in colour and well structured, that may only be bottled between the 4th and 6th year after the harvest. This extended period of time during which it can be bottled enables each producer to choose to bottle his wine earlier on or to wait until the very last moment to bottle it so to enable the wine to acquire some oxidation. The purpose of the expression "Late Bottled" is used precisely to indicate that this wine is bottled much later than a classic Vintage Port.

LBV is a very deep red wine and as such must be stored in large vats to prevent any loss of colour or oxidation. Care is taken not to handle this wine too much and its quality

depends, as you would expect, on the quality of the harvest. A same year may produce both an LBV and a Vintage Port. The one does not exclude the other.

The history of LBV is relatively brief as it was in the early 1960's that Port shippers began, with some reservations, to wager on this category of Port. With this type of wine, even in non-Vintage years a producer is able to offer a lush, full bodied and frequently tannic wine that offers you immense pleasure when you drink it, a wine that encourages you to venture further and taste the jewel in the crown – Vintage Port.

LBV is well known today and some firms even produce more of this than any other type of Port. The British market is the largest consumer of this wine and I have no doubt that interest in LBV will soon enjoy a great expansion to other markets.

As this is a wine from a single harvest, you may quite rightly wonder how firms can always have a good LBV to offer the consumer. The answer to this question resides in the Douro region and its great diversity of microclimates. Many Port shippers, in addition to their own *quintas* (wine estates), also purchase grapes and wine from the many farmers in the region. When I say "many" farmers, I am speaking of the hundreds and even, in some cases, thousands of farmers who have traditionally supplied shippers with grapes and wine, generation after generation, the sole contract being a verbal agreement. Thus, shippers have a wide range from which to choose the wines that they will bottle as an LBV.

There are different types of LBV on the market today. The difference lies in the way the wine is treated before it is bottled. Some houses prefer not to filter the wine before it is bottled which means that they will throw a deposit over the years; furthermore, they are harsher, rougher and closer to the original wine. In these cases (but not always), the designation *Traditional* may also appear on the label. Other houses (the majority), prefer to stabilise and filter the wine before it is bottled so that it will not throw a deposit; although it will lose some of its strength and structure, it is smoother and easier to drink. There is a market for both types of LBV and it is up to you to choose the one you prefer.

The current changes that are being made to the authorised designations suggest that the descriptor *Traditional* may become permitted for LBVs that, after having been bottled during the 4th and 6th year after the harvest, have aged in bottle for a minimum of 3 years before they are sold.

The growth in the market for LBV is also related to the price at which it is sold. It is a wine of excellent quality that is sold at a very attractive price, much below that of a good table wine, even a good Douro table wine. You will always have a great deal from which to choose and I would recommend that you include both of the above types of LBV in your wine cellar. Filtered LBV is a wine that goes down easily, does not need to be decanted and can be drunk at any time. Traditional LBV requires decanting and deserves a modicum of ceremony, should not remain too long in bottle and is excellent when drunk after a meal with a mild, or even a blue, cheese.

Vintage – The Jewel in the Crown

Vintage is a black purple superior quality wine from a single year, recognised as such by the Port Wine Institute Panel of Tasters. To be classified as a Vintage, the wine must be bottled between the 2nd and 3rd year after it is made or, more specifically, between 1 July of the 2nd year and 31 December of the 3rd year.

When making a Vintage, the producer chooses wines that have a great depth of colour, are very full bodied, with a high, albeit still very closed, concentration of aromas and with the tannins that it needs if it is to spend many years in bottle. Obtaining all this from a single year does not really depend on Man or on his capacity and skill to blend and handle wines. Either Nature sees fit to endow a wine with these characteristics or it does not. Thus, Vintage is a gift from Nature and, as we know so well, Nature is not inclined to be always this bountiful and the quirks of the climate inevitably affect the harvest, year after year.

When a viticultural year has been good you may think that it would be a Vintage year. However, for a year to have gone well means that a set of factors have to come together, factors that do not always "follow the rules of fair play". For example, a good viticultural year is one in which flowering occurred without problems, fruit set was not affected by frost or hail, the grapes ripened over the usual 40 days without suffering any great differences in temperature, there was enough water in the subsoil to feed the vine during the hot summer months; the grapes had attained an excellent state of maturation at the time of the harvest; the September rains caused no rot, among many other little details.

It is understandable that, as a producer has to depend on the vagaries of Nature to declare a Vintage, he will only declare a few Vintages each decade. When, in one year, the majority of Port houses declare a Vintage we call this a general declaration. This century, a Vintage year was declared on an average of three to four times a decade and, sometimes, even less frequently as between 1985 and 1991 no Vintage was declared. An interesting fact is that, so far this century, no year ending in 9 has ever been widely declared as a Vintage year!

From the Novidade to the Vintage

Much has been written on the history of the first vintages. There is no agreement as to when the first ever Vintage was declared. One thing is certain, that even if there were Vintage years in the past, these wines were totally unlike the wines of today due to, among other reasons, the limited amount of grape spirit that was added to the wine. Prior to the end of the 18th century, the amount of grape spirit varied between 36 and 48 litres per pipe, far less than the present day 110 litres per pipe. It was not until the mid 19th century that the amount added came close to the present amount. The maximum of 110 litres was only set in 1970; earlier this was set at 100 litres. In 1976, the IVP again lowered the limit to 105

Vineyards following the curve of the land.

litres per pipe and finally, in 1978, it was again raised to 110 litres.

News of the first declarations comes to us from the far off year of 1734. In those days, better quality wines destined for export were called *feitoria*, or commercial, wines. Within that group, the most superior quality wines were called *Novidade* and these corresponded to the present designation of Vintage. Even after the name Vintage became commonplace, the name Novidade continued to be used, at least until the beginning of the 20th century.

Knowing that the Lower Corgo was the first region in the Douro in which Port was produced and that today this sub-region is better known for its standard quality Port, you can see why there is such a difference between Vintage Port of the past and that which is produced today.

There were other differences as well, such as the time that passed between when the wine was made and when it was bottled. In those days, the wine was shipped in cask to London where it was stored, still in casks, by the importers who would occasionally fine them with egg[1] whites prior to

1 Also used for red table wine, this method consists of pouring lightly beaten egg

Old bottles of Port.

bottling, sometimes one or two years afterward they had received them.

London bottling continued until relatively recently. Vintage 1970 was the last year to have been partly bottled in London; from then onwards, all Vintage has been bottled in Portugal. Even so, shipments of Port in bulk continued, with the container gradually replacing the cask, until it was finally stopped in 1997. From then onwards, Port could only be shipped in bottle, with the exception of Port for culinary and special purposes.

Declaration of the Vintage

After a winemaker finishes the harvest and begins to examine the first of the new wines, he may form an opinion as to their quality but he cannot yet say whether this will be a Vintage year or not. Why is that? For some unaccountable reason, yet one that has traditionally been proven sound, he must wait two winters and one summer to see how the wine will behave. Let me give you an example: after making his wine in the fall of 1997, the winemaker will have to wait throughout the winter of 1997, the summer of 1998 and the winter

whites into the casks. As the egg whites slowly drift downwards, they take all foreign matter and floating particles with them, thus leaving the wine bright and clear. Also called "clarifying" the wine.

of 1998, until the spring of 1999, before he knows whether the wine is of Vintage quality or not. Over this period of time there occur a series of phenomena that cannot always be explained scientifically: the wines go through strange phases: they may lose their colour, their aromas, their strength. Then, after enduring the cold of two winters and the heat of one summer, they unaccountably regain all their earlier properties. It is then, and only then, that the winemaker blends his wines and decides whether or not he will declare it as a Vintage.

All producers have an additional advantage on their side when they declare a Vintage such a long time after the wine has been made. At this time, (spring 1999, for our example) he already has an idea, albeit not totally exact, as to the quality of the wine that was made the year after the wine in question and he can use this quality as a yardstick against which to measure the wine he is considering declaring. In other words, his decision to declare a Vintage may be checked against the possibility that the younger wine may also be of Vintage quality as some firms feel that one should avoid declaring a Vintage in successive years. An example of this occurred with Vintage 1991 which was generally declared by most firms; the overwhelming majority of which did not declare the 1992 wine. A few firms, however, did not accept the majority decision, preferring to declare only a Vintage 1992.

The above examples do not represent a set rule as there have been decades, such as the '80s, when more than an average of three Vintages per decade were declared. I don't really know why firms must respect the average of three declarations per decade; why not declare as often as is justified by the quality of the wine? These traditions, however, continue to weigh heavily on the Port Wine trade and there is no apparent desire to change these practices.

The timing of the declaration of a Vintage is absolutely crucial to the prestige of a Port house. Any mistake at this time may result in the massive loss of trade or, as so often happens, a decreased demand for other wines shipped by the same firm, even those of a standard quality. For example, on an average, the volume of sales of Vintage represent less than 5% of all the Port sold by a shipper, although it is those 5% that will reinforce the prestige of the firm's name and its future sales of all types of Port. This is why declaration of a Vintage is such a difficult decision, one that must be taken with the greatest of care.

It is at this time that the atmosphere in the Vila Nova de Gaia tasting rooms becomes one of great solemnity. There, on tables next to large windows made of the finest glass, facing North and overlooking the River Douro and the city of Porto on the other bank, the winemaker places the samples of the wines that might be included in the final blend. Vintage is almost always a blend of several wines produced in lesser or greater amounts: wines of a single year from several quintas, purchased from farmers or made in a firm's own winery from grapes purchased from farmers.

What the winemaker has to do is evaluate the intrinsic quality of each sample and not be influenced by its source. When he tastes these, the winemaker does not know whether a

Blending in the tasting room.

A vintage cellar in a lodge.

sample is from a lot of 1000 or 5000 litres. Naturally, all firms do not necessarily work this way, but it is the norm and the objective is always: not to favour quantity to the detriment of quality and to maintain the house style. It is not easy to define just what is a house style and it appears that there is an increasingly reduced range of styles. Until the '90s, one often spoke of a "British-style" Vintage as opposed to the style of Vintage produced by Portuguese firms. At the time, the main difference between these two was that the former had a characteristic austerity and harshness whilst the latter tended to be sweeter and easier to drink. I personally believe that the major differences began to disappear with Vintage 91 and were even less apparent with Vintages 94 and 95. The extensive tasting I have made of these suggests that today the predominant trend is for a British-style Vintage as this style is undoubtedly preferred in foreign markets, particularly new markets for Vintage such as the USA. I would say that a certain change in style is a response to new trends in the taste of the consumer.

You must not forget, also, that a taste for young vintages is a recent "fashion" and consumers are preferring new wines which, in spite of their harshness, can be drunk while still presenting the force of their youth. As regards style and in terms of the years in which a Vintage was generally declared, I would say that 1985 marked the end of an era and 1991 the beginning of new one. Vintage 85 still showed great differences in style between wines and there were discernible variations in quality; these initial differences were to become more marked as the wine aged in bottle. With Vintage 91, there was a sharp increase in average quality, itself very high, and few wines fell below this benchmark.

Once the winemaker has decided which lot of wine best expresses the quality and the house style he is looking for, the firm will send samples to the IVP Panel of Tasters who will then decide whether to approve the sample as a Vintage or not.

Approving a wine as a Vintage two years after it has been made necessarily requires considerable knowledge and experience in the Port Wine trade. The fact is, as Vintage is a wine that is going to spend many years in bottle to age, the winemaker must have an exact idea of which aromas a young wine must contain if it to attain the desired stage after so long in bottle. This is why certain fundamental aspects of a young Vintage must be taken into account. The main factor is colour: this must definitely be opaque and extremely concentrated if it is to still show a good red some 50 years later. The second vital factor are the tannins: the tannins must be clearly apparent and the wine may even be a bit harsh; should it be too soft, the wine will not survive long in bottle and be considered a Vintage without a future. It is, however, as regards the aromas that Vintage differs considerably from table wines, as contradictory as this may appear to be. In a young Vintage, the fact that the bouquet is initially very closed is not too serious a problem. In fact, the wine is most often very closed, with few obvious aromas, although you can denote the presence of red fruit. There are other aromas that are highly appreciated and which develop very well in the future, such as gum cistus (rock rose) and iodine. It is usually after some 10 to 15 years after the harvest that the aromas of a Vintage open up with a burst of ripe fruit and whose complexity is at the heart of this unique wine, one without parallel worldwide.

Once the IVP has approved a Vintage, it issues the guarantee seals that will be placed on each bottle. The producer must inform the Institute exactly how much wine he intends to bottle and this will be recorded in the current wine account that the IVP has for each firm.

In years when most houses declare a Vintage, shippers become almost festive. As a gesture of fellowship, firms send samples of their wine to their competitors which means that an enormous number of bottles travel from firm to firm, marking an end to the Vintage "hostilities". Obviously this is not a case of open warfare but rather a period of great contention between firms as to whether to declare or not. Each firm is a quite closed, small world that rarely admits the presence of someone from another firm. It is not unusual to hear a shipper state that he has never visited one or another competitor's installations. This secrecy is difficult to understand considering that there are no secrets as how these wines are made or cared for nor can you say that the house style is exactly displayed at the entrance, which is why a stranger is less perceptive of this climate. This is the way it has been for centuries and, from what I know of the trade, will continue to be so.

There is, though, a time when this secrecy is essential: when it becomes time to decide whether to declare a Vintage or not. If a firm declares and no one else does, or very few other firms do, there is a certain feeling of isolation that is far from beneficial to the wine as regards its standing on the market. If practically no firms declare, it is usually because this was not an excellent year overall and one cannot set a high price for the wine that was declared. If, on the other hand, almost everyone declares and only one or two firms do not, the market may think that this is because their wine is less good which may also adversely affect their sales.

With this "damned if you do and damned if you don't" situation, firms try to find out what the majority of other shippers intend to do so as to avoid taking an isolated decision. At first, everyone plays his cards close to his chest and no one makes the first move; then as rumours start circulating on the grapevine and a few off the record remarks are made, one becomes aware of a rising feeling of anticipation that only ends when the IVP publishes its approvals. After all, it was not enough to have decided to declare a Vintage. The winemaker had to decide what type of Vintage the firm was going to submit for approval.

SINGLE QUINTA VINTAGE

Knowing that the Douro region is so rich in microclimates and in different zones where many different types of wine can be produced during a same vintage, you could rightly say that practically every year is potentially a Vintage year. In better years there will always be a greater amount of Vintage but even in less abundant years, some wine will always be submitted for approval. Very rarely do you see a year in which no single shipper or producer-bottler declares a Vintage, not even under a second-line brand. 1969, 81 and 93 were disastrous years overall but even so, at least one firm each year produced some wine that it declared.

What can a firm do during those years when the quality falls below the highest standards? There are several possible solutions: forget the tradition of only declaring three Vintage years each decade and declare a Vintage whenever the grapes produce a superior quality wine that meets the standards; downgrade the wine from Vintage and make an LBV; or opt for an increasingly popular solution, decide to declare a second-line Single Quinta Vintage, to use a description that has become commonplace in the trade.

A Single Quinta Vintage is a wine whose label usually bears the name of the quinta on which the grapes that went into its making were grown, contrary to the finest years when a classic Vintage is declared, when the Vintage bears the firm's name. That which distinguishes a Single Quinta from a classic, top-of-the-range Vintage is that the wine is usually less full-bodied, more easily drunk when young and is not likely to last as long in bottle. This downgrading of a Vintage has nothing to do with the quality of the wine which remains of superior quality. If it were not so, it would never be approved by the IVP. The Panel of Tasters does not approve a wine according to the importance it is given by a firm; it does not even know whether the wine it is approving will be declared as a classic or a Single Quinta Vintage. All the Panel of Tasters is interested in is whether the wine meets the stipulated standards of quality for a Vintage Port or not.

These wines offer several advantages to the consumer, the main one being the enormous difference in price between a Single Quinta and a classic Vintage. With a Single Quinta, you are offered an excellent wine for less money, that you can drink when it is younger, all of which is sufficiently attractive to explain the great demand there is for these wines.

Having said this, there are two other possible situations: these Vintages may not necessarily bear the name of a quinta but you can still easily distinguished them according to the name that appears on the label, even if it not the firm's main name. Let me give you two examples, taken at random: Graham's second-line Vintage is bottled under the name of Malvedos. The word "quinta" does not appear on the label but neither does "Graham" as the latter is reserved exclusively for its top Vintage Ports; Fonseca's also does not use the name "quinta", preferring Guimaraens as a sub-brand, reserving "Fonseca" for its finest wines.

There are, moreover, some years when some firms declare both a Quinta and a brand name Vintage, such as the case of Ferreira. In this case, the former is not a second-line wine but a true classic Vintage made from a single quinta.

In the latter group of special circumstances there are two additional situations: Vintages made by producers-bottlers who will naturally use the name of their quinta without intending to indicate that these are second-line wines; and Quinta do Vesúvio Vintage which is always made solely from grapes grown on that property and for which there is no sub-brand. In less excellent years, the wine is simply not bottled as a Vintage.

BUYERS OWN BRANDS (BOB)

Today, a significant amount of Port of all categories is bottled under the buyer's own brand (BOB). This is a new commercial trend that, as we have seen with other products, has also been adopted by the Port trade. This can create considerable confusion to the consumer who finds himself confronted

Douro lodge.

Pipes waiting to be unloaded – Vila Nova de Gaia.

with Ports under the most peculiar names or labelled under the name of a supermarket chain or that of the importer. Nevertheless, a careful look at the label should usually reveal the name of the producer; you can then determine whether the wine was made by a firm you know and like.

You might have the impression that all these BOB wines are always of poorer quality than those sold under the so-called "authentic" names. One should not draw such a hasty conclusion as there is much BOB of excellent quality and it does have an additional advantage – it is often sold at a considerably more attractive price.

Baron Forrester.

3. More than 300 Years
of History

Port is made on the hillsides overlooking the River Douro and in the valleys and hillsides of its tributaries. The Douro Region was already producing wine well before Portugal became a nation, that is, prior to the 12th century. We know today that vines were cultivated in this mountainous region in prehistoric times and also that the Romans, during their occupation of the Iberian Peninsula, encouraged viticulture. Although blessed with a unique soil and climate in the region, the planting and care of vineyards in this region is so difficult that winemaking has forever been a daunting challenge for the people of the Douro.

Following Portugal's declaration of independence from Spain in the 12th century, there was a clear development of viticulture in the Douro. The inclusion of viticulture in the list of products mentioned in the Royal Town Charters is witness to the importance given to wine at a time when currency, as a means of exchange, was rare. Entire communities would pay their taxes with wine, a practice that became customary throughout the kingdom. In Medieval times, wine, together with cereals and olive oil, represented one of the pillars of rural economies and one of the Crown's principle sources of income. The climate in the region is not only propitious to wine. Other crops such as almonds and olives also thrive in its Mediterranean-like climate. Even today, the people of the Douro are extremely proud of their almonds, which they serve with White Port, and their olive oil, considered one of the finest in Portugal.

The movement that led to the expulsion of the Moors, who had come from Africa to occupy the Iberian Peninsula, began in the North and rapidly extended to the South where

Stained glass window - Casa do Douro, Régua.

there also were vineyards, in spite of the fact that the Koran prohibited Moslems from drinking wine. Wine was drunk by the Christians who continued to live in occupied territory, which explains why even in the Middle Ages, vineyards were to be found from the north to the south of Portugal.

The first records of wine exported in any substantial quantity from the Douro region date back as far as the 13th century, France being the first country to import Douro wine. Historians do not, however, believe that production was all that widespread or that it had any significant impact on the local economy at that time. The Douro Region was always very poor and underdeveloped, the countryside was primarily covered with scrub and the people lived from what they could scrounge from the land and from hunting; the little agriculture that existed was purely for subsistence. Furthermore, the extreme isolation forced upon human habitations by the mountains that rise around the River Douro, restricted trade between this and other regions.

The history of this region is inevitably associated to that of its wine. One might even say that the 18th century is the dividing line of two, very different eras. Prior to this, the history of wine in the region was of such little importance that there was not much worth recording. Vines had always been planted here and there on tiny plots of land and the people had always lived most precariously. With rare exceptions, there were no aristocratic habitations or any sign of large, wealthy communities that might have been seriously interested in wine.

It was only in the land that surrounded monasteries, such as São João de Tarouca near Lamego, that wine production attained values that we can consider of interest, not only in terms of the amount that was made but also in terms of the final destination of the wine. There are 16th century docu-

A Vintage in the 1940's.

ments that mention 750 pipes of wine (each pipe contains 550 litres) produced from monastery vineyards, all destined for export.

In the 18th century, however, everything changed: the pattern of rural economics underwent a massive change, the landscape was totally modified and social relationships became transformed. Nevertheless, some traces of the past remain to this day and the countryside still bears scars of the extreme poverty of the past.

PORTO MERCHANTS AND SHIPPERS

There was an enormous impetus to the production of wine in the 18th century, much of which due to the wars that since the second half of the 17th century had opposed the French and British kings. One of the results of this rivalry was that the French promptly upped taxes on Bordeaux wines shipped to England where they were greatly appreciated. Charles II responded by decreeing a boycott on the importation of these wines. Consequently, British merchants began look-

Ships in Vila Nova de Gaia.

ing elsewhere for wines to replace those they could no longer import from France and their attentions very rapidly lit upon Portugal and, most especially, its wine.

It was the shortage of wine in England that was finally responsible for the rapidly rising exports of Portuguese wines during the second half of the 17th century. A major contributing factor to this expansion was the Treaty of Methuen-Alegrete of Dec 27 1703 by which British wool and woollens were to be admitted into Portugal duty-free, and Portuguese wine to be admitted into England at a greatly reduced rate – 2/3 of the rate charged on French wines.

Much has been written in Portugal about the advantages and disadvantages of this treaty but there is no doubt whatsoever that, from this date onwards, there was an enormous upsurge of viticulture in this country. There was a sudden interest in wine production and many farms that had been planted with cereal crops and fruit trees were turned into vineyards. What actually happened would not, to a certain extent, be exactly beneficial to the Douro. The French competitor had been eliminated but the market was invaded by Portuguese competitors from other regions who took advantage of the prestige of these wines from the North and their fame on the British market. Agricultural monoculture took over in the Douro region as prices soared and more and more farmers decided to abandon all other crops and dedicate themselves exclusively to viticulture and winemaking.

Soon, the glut of wine that followed sent prices plummeting downwards. To give you an example, the price of 60 000 *reis* fetched by a pipe of wine after the Treaty of Methuen dropped, by the middle of the 18th century, to 6 000 *reis* per pipe. The government intervened with a view to controlling a market that had gotten completely out of hand; one of the results was the demarcation of the Douro winemaking region as part of the agricultural reform policy of the Marquis of Pombal, minister to Joseph I who for 25 years (1750-1775) reigned over Portugal.

BRITISH MERCHANTS IN PORTUGAL

Portuguese and British still frequently refer to the ancient alliance that brought both countries together. Early links were mainly commercial and date back to the 14th century, with a first trade agreement in 1353. On May 9 1386 England and Portugal became permanently allied with the signing, by Kings John I of Portugal and Richard II of England, of the Treaty of Windsor which established the foundations for privileged trading relations and mutual assistance between the two monarchies. After King John married Philippa of Lancaster, the daughter of John of Gaunt, in 1387, the Portuguese dynasty became partly English.

From then onwards, commercial relations between both countries and the establishment of British merchants in Portugal, namely in Porto and Viana, grew continuously. Prior to the 17th century, the British were more interested in trading salt from Aveiro and goods from the Portuguese colonies such as Brazilian sugar and tobacco. Fisheries and the salting of codfish also interested them, even before they turned their attentions to the wines from the Alto Minho and the Douro.

The activities of the British merchants were made considerably easier following the treaty John IV of Portugal and Charles I of England signed in 1642. A growing number of British merchants settled in Portugal, many who were to dedicate themselves to the increasingly important wine trade between both countries. Although the first recorded exports of Portuguese wine from the North of Portugal to England are dated 1651, the year of 1678 when 405 pipes of wine were shipped, is the first year for which we have an annual figure. It appears that these wines were undoubtedly a blend of wines from several regions: Douro, Anadia (Bairrada), Viana (Vinho Verde) and Lisbon.

Although there were many fewer British merchants in Porto than there were Portuguese, the fact that the former traded mainly in wine, a product with a greater intrinsic value which they exported, led them to leadership in this sector. Between 1745 and 1756, British wine merchants (whose number fluctuated occasionally but always remained at around 30) were responsible for about 60% of the city's trade in wine, whereas Portuguese merchants, whose number was more stable and varied between 70 and 90, only controlled about 35% of the business. The remaining 5% was in the hands of German, French and Dutch merchants..

The Marquis of Pombal.

A WINE SHAPED BY THE BRITISH TASTE

From the very beginning, the British showed considerable interest in this new product. What they particularly liked was the wine's deep colour and power, fruit of burning hot summers where temperatures often rose above 40°C. As the wine was sent to London in wooden casks, it was not infrequently "treated" before it was shipped to prevent its going off during the sea voyage. At first, only a little brandy – approximately 20 litres per pipe – was added. This was, to some extent, the first step towards making the type of Port we know today although producers were far from a general consensus of opinion as to the style of the wine that would later become famous as Port Wine. The name the Portuguese gave to this wine changed several times before they settled on the term that is used today: *vinho fino* (meaning quality wine, was first used in 1607 and applied to both white and red wines, but never to Vinho Verde wines); *vinho generoso* (fortified wine); *vinho de embarque* (shipping wine); *vinho do Douro* (Douro wine); *vinho de feitoria* (commercial wine); *vinho de carregação* (wine to be loaded). Of all these, only *vinho fino* survives to this day.

The first time that the expression Port Wine appears in Portuguese documents dates to 1675 when Duarte Ribeiro de Macedo[2], in a discussion on wine exported to Holland, speaks of a *Vinho do Porto*. This designation was most probably given in reference to all the wine that was shipped across the bar of the River Douro at Porto and not especially to wine from the Douro. In time, the *Vinho do Porto*, or Port Wine, stuck and although everyone knows that this wine is made in the Douro, this has become the official designation. In deference to local tradition, *Vinho Fino*, only employed by Douro farmers when referring to the fortified wine they pro-

---

2 Diplomat and writer who defended introducing industry into Portugal, in line with the commercial ideas that were so fashionable in Europe at the time.

duce, the one they consider to be their "own" Port Wine, is also accepted in the region.

SWEET OR DRY WINE?

Initially, the wine was not sweet. Adding sugar (or a fortified wine) to the wine fermenting in the vats was a practice that developed from the British taste for strong, deeply coloured, sweet wines. In order to obtain the very deep purple black colour that British merchants wanted, farmers often resorted to adding crushed elderberries. This fruit was picked in the Douro and the Beira Alta regions where elderberries grew in great profusion; very deep red in colour, the berries added considerably to the colour of the wine.

At the same time that farmers were making these very sweet wines, they continued to make the traditional dry Douro wines, also called Port.

The debate as to which wine best represented the "Port type" went on and on and lasted until well into the 19th century. Those who ardently defended the traditional wines, led by the Baron Forrester, preferred dry wines "with little or no brandy added", whilst others defended the sweet wines. We know today that the decision as to how the Port we know today should be made was not taken on any specific date. There was the evident historic British influence which had the final say as to the style of the wine – sweet, deep purple black and full bodied – yet the steps taken to reach this were slow and irregular. Several sources refer to 1820 as a benchmark in creating the type of wine that would be called Port. That year, the wine was especially full-bodied, lush and sweet and it was this model that winemakers tried to recreate in the following years. There very well might have been some influence from the Sherry region of Southern Spain as in those days, brandy was already being added to Sherry and this technique was not totally unknown to those British merchants who were likewise connected to that trade.

In the 17th century, the blooming British merchant community in the North of Portugal met regularly near the quay in Porto to discuss the exchange and transact business. By

Baron Forrester

the end of the 18th century, the venue of choice was the new
Factory House[3], built by merchants from all sectors of com-
merce. This tradition continues to this day although mem-
bership of the British Association as it is also known, is restricted to male members of British Port firms who meet each

---

3 Standing, at first, for every english business man, after the Napoleonic Wars, in
  the XIX century, the Factory House was restrained to Port Wine merchants.

Wednesday over lunch. (Until quite recently, women were not even allowed to enter the building by the main entrance, let alone breach the exclusively male business lunches!)

The honour of being the Oldest Port Wine House falls to Köpke, founded in 1638. Warre (1670) is next, followed by Croft (1678). Then there is a long list of firms, many of whom are still well known today: Quarles Harris (1680); Taylor, Fladgate & Yeatman (1692); Morgan Brothers (1715); Offley Forrester (1729); Butler & Nephew (1730); Hunt Roope (1735) and Sandeman (1790), to name but a few. During the first hundred years, the trade was totally dominated by British merchants who were occasionally linked to traders from other countries in Central Europe, such as Dutch or German.

The so-called primacy of the British in the Port trade has been a frequent thorn in the side of the many Portuguese merchants who also operate in this sector and who played an important role in its development in spite of the fact that the majority of exporters were British. Many period paintings and illustrations (especially during the 19th century) tend to indicate that it was the British who were exclusively responsible for selling this wine. Those who espoused this somewhat simplistic view believed that the world of Port was divided into two distinct groups which, although complementary, represented two opposing interests: the farmers and the British. Recent studies by both Portuguese and foreign historians have demonstrated what the trade itself has always known, which is that from the onset there were a great many Portuguese merchants who either operated and shipped under their own labels or served as a link between the two parties. Unfortunately, we do not have the names of these earliest Portuguese traders nor are they indicated in the Customs and Excise records of the period, yet their role both in the capital market and in the trade was of undoubted importance.

DEMARCATION OF THE DOURO REGION

As a result of the great demand from abroad for the wine from the region, there was a rapid increase in the amount of land under vines during the first half of the 18th century.

Unfortunately, this uncontrolled expansion of vineyards and the absence of any boundaries to the area in which Port could be made meant that vineyards in regions far distant from the Douro began to produce grapes that were later also made into Port. On the other hand, the British taste for sweet wines led many farmers to adulterate their product by adding sugar, using poor quality brandy and increasing amounts of elderberries. British merchants accused the farmers of being responsible for the consequent poor quality but these insisted that it was the shippers who were falsifying the wine they exported by adding inferior quality wine from other regions to the wine from the Douro. In the middle of all this debate, the mid-1800s were affected by a succession of poor farming years that resulted in very poor quality wine. The resulting shortage of wine for export further encouraged firms to resort to wine from outside the Douro region.

The stage was set for the government's absolutist and interventionist policies – a political model followed by Joseph I and implemented by his minister, the Marquis of Pombal who would take a firm hand and try to put this chaotic situation in order, namely by creating a controlling entity that would be the hallmark of the State's involvement in the Port trade.

It was in such circumstances that in 1756, a group of notables in the Kingdom led by Frei João de Mansilha and Bartolomeu Pancorbo, supported by the Marquis of Pombal, created the *Companhia Geral da Agricultura das Vinhas do Alto Douro*, or Companhia for short.

The objectives of the Companhia were clear: encourage the cultivation of the vine in the Alto Douro, safeguard the authenticity of the product and control its price. Another pressing issue it would address was the monopoly of the British who, due to their dominant position in this sector, ended up by dictating the laws of supply and demand regardless of the opinions of the farmers.

Meanwhile, the authenticity of the product could not be controlled unless one knew exactly which were the areas where Port could or could not be made. In other words, unless the region were to be demarcated, it would be impossible for the Companhia to ensure that the grapes would come from the appropriate regions within the Douro. At that time the trade already had a clear idea of the range in the quality of wine, particularly that made within this particular region. This is why from the onset, the very first demarcation refers to two types of wine: commercial, or *feitoria*, wines of better quality especially destined for export and ordinary, or *ramo*, wines of inferior quality only sold on the domestic market.

The government commissioned a map of the region that would indicate the boundaries of the areas in which feitoria wine could be made. It is interesting to note that this map included some land belonging to Frei João de Mansilha although it was perhaps not the best for making Port...

Thus, the first demarcated wine region in the world was born. Many countries, namely in Central Europe, claim that they too had areas that were clearly identified as authorised regions in which a wine with special characteristics might be produced. This may be so, but the very first demarcation to include a classification of the vineyards and of the different quality wines produced therein was, without a shadow of a doubt, the one applied to the Douro winemaking region.

The demarcation did not occur all at once. Initially the area that was considered best for superior quality wines was that of the Lower Corgo that extended from the eastern border as far as Pinhão. In following years, this region was extended through a series of royal charters that increased the area recognised as suitable for producing the superior quality feitoria wine for export.

With a view to guarantee the quality of the wine, the Companhia imposed a series of rules and prohibitions: it banned the use of farmyard manure in vineyards; separation of red and white grapes became compulsory; the addition of elderberries to the wine was prohibited and all elderberry bushes growing within a 5 league radius of the river were ripped out. Later, the ban on elderberry bushes was extended to much more distant regions such as the provinces of the Minho, Trás-os-Montes and Beira Alta. In 1765, the Marquis of Pombal ordered the destruction of all vines planted on land traditionally devoted to the cultivation of rice and grain in the Mondego, Vouga and Tagus

The Douro Demarcated Region.

river valleys. Thus, the government attempted to protect the production of wine in the Douro and make it more difficult for grapes from other regions to be brought illegally into the region, a phenomenon that was evident in years when little wine was made.

As to the wine itself, the vineyards were classified according to the type of wine they produced. There were two basic types of wine: commercial, or *feitoria*, wines of better quality especially destined for export; and ordinary, or *ramo*, wines of inferior quality only shipped to Brazil or sold on the domestic market in the event of a lack of quality, or *vinho fino*, wine. This was then followed by five types of wine whose price was set according to their quality.

So that there may remain no doubts as to which vineyards were and which were not located within the Demarcated Douro Region, granite markers or milestones were placed along the boundaries in 1758. From then onwards, no wine was admitted to the region without its respective documents. This way, the government strove to safeguard the authenticity of the wine entitled to bear the Denomination of Origin, applying severe punishments to all offenders.

Granite boundary marker.

When you look at the current map of the Demarcated Douro Region you will note that the present area is much greater than the one first demarcated under the Marquis of Pombal. A series of later demarcations continued until well into the 20th century at the same time as the concept itself of what a quality wine should be, changed. Today there are highly sought after areas where Port is produced that were not even included in the original map. Although the concept of a registry of vineyards remained constant, it was only in the 30s and 40s that detailed classification standards were established with a great deal of precision.

The Companhia, as the government entity was generally

known, enjoyed certain privileges, some of which of vital importance to the quality of Port such as its monopoly over the sale of the grape spirit used to fortify the wine and its exclusivity over the sale of ordinary, or *ramo*, wine in the city of Porto. The issue of the monopoly over the sale of the grape spirit was to prove of vital importance given that the use of very poor quality brandy had become widespread during the rapid growth in the trade in the second half of the 18th century. This was, in fact, one of the main complaints firms had against farmers whom they accused of falsifying the wine with extremely poor brandy. Even today, this spirit is very carefully chosen although, contrary to what one might think, it need not come from the region or even from Portugal. As this is a neutral grape spirit, its actual origin does not influence the typical characteristics of the wine it is used to fortify.

The Companhia did not have an easy time. On the one hand it was the steel glove that represented the power of the throne and corresponded to the notion of economic intervention defended by the Marquis of Pombal. This, during the second half of the 18th century, long before the appearance of the more liberal doctrine that the market would adopt as the best means of controlling the trade. On the other hand, the Companhia was widely hated as it was responsible for enforcing strict rules of behaviour for all economic agents, dictating everything from the methods to be used in winemaking to the final price for which the wine was to be sold. The more numerous the prohibitions, the more fertile the imagination of those who wish to infringe the law, and this second half of the century abounded in laws that imposed heavy penalties for anyone who attempted to breach the strict legal controls imposed by the Companhia.

AFTER THE MARQUIS OF POMBAL

With the death of Joseph I (1777), the Marquis of Pombal lost his seat in the government and his power. The first move of the new government ministers in the total remodelling of the Companhia that followed, was to rescind some of the Companhia's privileges. Less strict control in the region resulted in an unrestrained rise in exports, probably fruit of mixing ordinary wine with the superior quality wine for export. In 1776 exports attained 20,000 pipes; one year later, after the fall of the Marquis, this amount shot up to 27,000 pipes.

The authorities were then faced with a major dilemma as they were forced to choose between, on the one hand, adopting a more liberal policy that would make trading easier and allow for a freer circulation of goods and, on the other hand, the need to guarantee a minimum of income for the State Treasury through the Companhia's activities. This explains why, in spite of much criticism against it, the Companhia was never totally extinguished and it only suffered the loss of some of its privileges.

The last quarter of the 18th century was a period of some confusion as the more flexible administration that succeeded the Marquis of Pombal's rule of iron made life easier for those who were counterfeiting Port. Meanwhile, the international

Pipe's load ready for the trip to Oporto.

political situation also gave a great boost to the Port trade – the French Revolution and the state of war between France and England favoured exports from Portugal as the wine was shipped by sea and England ruled the waves. By the end of the century, exports reached an astronomic 100,000 pipes, although the average for the period from 1777 to 1810 was approximately 28,000 pipes per year. At the beginning of the 19th century, Port represented about 80% of all Portuguese wine exported although this trading supremacy gradually waned as a result of increasing exports of table wine, namely to Brazil.

There followed a period of great prosperity in the Douro: new quintas were planted and many stately homes and churches were refurbished. Minor adjustments were made to the demarcated region and you begin to see a greater acceptance of the wines from the Upper Corgo, to the detriment of those from the Lower Corgo.

Portugal underwent a period of considerable political unrest during the first 20 years of the 19th century with the invasion of the French troops under Napoleon and the Royal Family and the Court's fleeing to Brazil, the rising British military and political presence in the country and in 1820, the fall of the Absolutist Monarchy. Naturally, the Port trade suffered and exports rose and fell dramatically during this entire period. The Companhia continued to be the prime target of all those who espoused commercial freedom. Approximately 40% of all economic treatises published between 1820 and 1838 were directed against the Companhia Geral das Vinhas do Alto Douro.

By then, most of the British firms in the Port trade had become firmly established and many of them continue to trade under the same names today. This sector was not fertile in the appearance of new operators and, even in the 20th century, there were very few totally new Port houses.

THE 19TH CENTURY – BEFORE AND AFTER THE PHYLLOXERA

With the advent of the Liberal movement (1820) and the new social structure that followed the end of the civil war, the Port trade embarked in new directions. Although the

Liberals did not have a global plan for the Douro and were under great pressure from the British who wanted freer trade, the government gradually altered the structure of the Companhia until it was abolished, for the first time, in 1834. Re-established in 1838, the Companhia was again re-organised in 1843 only to be extinguished, once and for all, in 1863. Its existence marked the history of the Port trade, for better or worse, and the issue of the Companhia still has the power to engender passionate debates. Always a vehicle of an interventionist government and the permanent focus of conflicts between farmers and merchants, at all times, however, it represented the supervisory entity that designed and constructed the foundations for a great structure that proved capable of surviving all the natural and social avalanches of the past two hundred years: the Port Wine trade.

As the Companhia's iron hand was replaced by the Liberal government's kid gloves, fraud spread and prospered: elderberries were again added to the wine, much more good and bad wines were mixed together; more productive varieties of vines were planted; excessively sweet fortified wines were added to table wine to make a type of Port; wines from other regions were brought into Vila Nova de Gaia where, meanwhile, shippers were beginning to enlarge their lodges.

Because of this climate of total viticultural anarchy, the Companhia was re-established in 1838. Unfortunately, this remake suffered from the same evil of all other remakes: rarely is one an improvement over the original. The so-called "new" Companhia was stripped of most of its responsibilities and it never regained its controlling authority. Not surprisingly, the new version only lasted 20 years and until its demise in 1863, never managed to be more than a very pale shadow of the authoritarian entity created by the Marquis of Pombal.

This entire period (until 1851) was marked by massive production and a general drop in prices, the natural outcome of the great many new vineyards planted without control or attention to quality. By the mid 19th century, the entire trade had fallen into disrepute and it would take a natural calamity to bring production back under control: oidium[4].

---

4 Fungus that destroys the bunches of grapes and, if untreated, of the vine itself.

Mortuaries – abandoned vineyards.

This plague, which took ten years to be effectively checked, caused the ruin of many farmers although it did not affect exports. In spite of the massive decrease in production, generally by half, exports actually rose in significant amounts. This was a period of farmers abandoning the land and of the reorganisation of the productive sector, clearly demonstrating that in times of natural catastrophes, it was the farmers and not the shippers who suffered the most.

The Douro had only barely recovered from the oidium when it was struck by a second plague, the phylloxera[5], which infested and decimated practically all the vineyards in the region. The first vineyards to be contaminated by this nematode were detected in 1868 and the plague rapidly spread over the entire region.

Numerous attempts were made to resolve the problem, some of which really belonged to the realm of the fantastic. The sole possible way to combat the plague was to plant American vines that were apparently immune to attack and as yet there is still no way to eradicate this nematode, today

Treated with sulphur. Develops more rapidly under certain weather conditions, namely when days of intense heat follow several days of rain. (Usually in May/June).

5 Nematode that attacks and destroys the roots of the vine. This plague was only controlled by planting rootstock that is impervious to this microscopic insect.

Caring for a
vineyard.

The 19th century
was fertile in
texts concerning
the crisis in the
Douro.

almost all the vineyards continue to be planted with selected domestic vines grafted onto American rootstock.

No sooner had farmers begun to replant their vineyards that a new plague hit the region in 1893: mildew. Fortunately not as destructive as the phylloxera, it was more easily controlled. Spraying of the Bordeaux Mixture, based on sulphur, proved effective in combating this disease.

These three plagues forced the total restructuring of the Douro vineyards. Whilst this greatly affected the farmers, it had less of an effect on the trade. The existence of large stocks of wine enabled firms to sustain, and even increase, their shipments of Port. Furthermore, as the phylloxera had first destroyed the French vineyards before attacking Portugal, our wines (from the Douro and other winemaking regions in the country) had no difficulty in finding buyers. With so many people wanting to purchase wine and the increasing rarity of quality wine, it was almost inevitable that unscrupulous merchants would again adulterate the wine, mixing wine from the south and selling it as Port and fortifying it with ordinary alcohol instead of brandy. In the end, it was the Porto merchants who benefited from the crisis as they extended their area of influence within the region itself by purchasing quintas and investing in vineyards. By the end of the 19th century, exports were again approaching record levels as shipments again came close to a total one hundred thousand pipes.

From the moment the phylloxera appeared, the social organisation and the relationships between the various groups involved in the region were to undergo a complete change. The people of the Douro were the ones who by far paid the highest price for the crisis as over a short period of time, the twenty years that passed between the appearance of the phylloxera and the solution to this plague, they no longer had any grapes or wine to sell and vast areas under vine were abandoned. These old vineyards are still known today by a most appropriate name: mortuaries. Hillsides scarred by deserted terraces are still visible to those who travel along the banks of the River Douro.

As ruined farmers and landowners abandoned vineyards *en masse*, new groups with sufficient wealth to invest in the

Douro appeared on the Port scene. Many quintas changed hands, new vineyards were planted and interest in the Douro intensified. Many firms that before had been solely engaged in exporting Port began to invest in property in the Douro and the Porto bourgeoisie showed an increasing interest in the Douro vineyards, the landscape was transformed as use of the American rootstock led to the reformulation of the techniques for planting a vineyard and the laying out of the terraces, and the Port trade gained new impetus.

The demarcated region grew in size as the River Douro became navigable as far as the Spanish border and the railway line was extended to the Upper Douro. This latter region became known as a producer of superior quality wines that were becoming increasingly famous. During the second half of the 19th century, there appeared new quintas that remain famous to this day, such as Vesúvio, Vargellas and Monte Meão. The advent of the railway shortened distances and

Old, pre-phylloxera treading tank.

The crisis seen by Rafael Bordalo Pinheiro.

improved transport, especially that of wine from the quintas to the Gaia lodges.

The effect of these plagues was also felt at the level of the agricultural practices. From then onwards, treatment against mildew and against oidium became obligatory and the need to graft domestic vines on the imported rootstock required the careful selection of the vines that would be used for grafting. Although the Port merchants had not suffered from the crisis thanks to their surplus stocks of wine, the production of Vintage Ports – those with the greatest prestige –

naturally underwent a hiatus given that very few vineyards were producing grapes. It was only at the end of the 19th century, most precisely in 1896, that you again hear speak of good quality wines, made from grapes grown on the new, post-phylloxera vineyards, the new vineyards that had meanwhile been planted only began producing grapes at the beginning of the 1890s.

There are some shippers today who still have some pre-phylloxera wine in their cellars and they often make *before* and *after* comparisons. As regards the style of the wines made before the phylloxera, there is only one such type of wine that continues to this day although it is almost beyond the reach of the average consumer due to the extremely high prices it fetches. This is a wine from Quinta do Noval called Vintage Nacional, precisely because it is made from ungrafted vines, that is, vines planted directly into the soil and not grafted onto American rootstock. Nacional is not a pre-phylloxera wine; it is a wine that is currently made from grapes grown on vineyards planted according to pre-phylloxera practices.

THE 20TH CENTURY

The Demarcated Douro Region was substantially enlarged at the beginning of the 20th century. First, in 1907, on the orders of the dictator João Franco who proposed a massive expansion of the region that soon became obviously excessive. Consequently, a new geographic outline was drawn up the following year. Aside from some minor adjustments to the boundaries in 1921, the authorised winemaking region of today corresponds roughly to the 1908 demarcation.

The government again intervened in the trade, not just for the purpose of protecting the international use of the denomination *Port* that was being indiscriminately applied by many merchants in other European countries, but also with a view to ensuring the permanent control of the quality and authenticity of Port at the domestic level, by creating the Viticultural Committee for the Douro Region. At the same time, demarcation began for other winemaking regions in

Wine being inspected by an IVP employee in Gaia, before unloading.

Portugal with special characteristics of their own, such as Dão, Vinho Verde, Bucelas and Carcavelos.

Throughout this century, the Douro region has been constantly assailed, with some reason, by a craving for protectionism and demands for state intervention on the one hand, and the desire for free trade on the other. It is interesting that it has always been under dictatorships (of different types and ideologies) that the government has enacted the legal - mechanisms for controlling the region. Several of the existing regulatory entities governing the sector - the Casa do Douro (1932), the Port Wine Institute (IVP) (1933) and the Guild of Port Shippers (1933) - were created during the period of the *Estado Novo* (a dictatorship that began in 1926 with a military coup). For more than 60 years, the Demarcated Douro Region endured a three-way relationship involving the State, represented by the IVP – the farmers, represented by the Casa do Douro – and the merchants who were members of the Guild of Port Shippers.

The seal of guarantee that is affixed on bottles and has been compulsory since 1942, was developed to guarantee the certification of origin and the authenticity of the wine. A special bonded area enclosing the shippers' lodges in Gaia and considered part of the Demarcated Region – the Gaia *Entreposto*, was also created. The purpose of this bonded area was to effect a tighter control on exports and on all wine sold as Port. As this wine could no longer be shipped directly from the Douro, all the wine exported became subject to strict government control[6]. In 1934, responsibility for controlling the quality of Port fell to a Panel of Tasters from the Port Wine Institute. A detailed survey of the region was carried out between 1937 and 1945 for purposes of organising the registry of vineyards. The system by which farmers were attributed licenses to make specific quantities of wine into Port was now based on parameters that had been scientifically studied by Álvaro Moreira da Fonseca (see page 108).

---

6 All the wines arriving from the Douro and destined for the lodges in Gaia were inspected upon entry to the *Entreposto*. All wines exported from the lodges were subject to control; the amount of wine shipped was then deducted from each company's current wine account with the Port Wine Institute.

Loadind in Gaia.

The ups and downs in the Port trade during the 20th century have been caused not only by the vagaries of nature but also by the effects of two world wars. Also this century, England lost its supremacy as the largest importer of Port, to France. From the onset, however, and contrary to the British market, the French market has always imported considerably inferior quality wines. As a result, there was an emergence of firms in the 1930s, whose sole interest was essentially that of shipping cheap Port to France. Once again the government intervened to stop this somewhat dubious trade by prohibiting the sale of Port below 16.5°C of alcohol and under a minimum of 2 years of age.

Further changes also occurred within Portugal. In 1964, the government authorised the transport of wine from the Douro to Porto by road (until then, this had to be done compulsory by train or boat) and wines gradually began to be exported in containers rather than in wooden casks. There was a notable increase in the percentage of bottled Port sold although most Vintage continued to be exported in bulk. It was only after Vintage 1970 that the government decreed that all Vintage Port had to be bottled in Portugal and only after 1 July 1996 that it suspended the export of all Port in bulk.

The Douro in the Upper Corgo.

The requirement that all Port had to be exported through the Gaia Entreposto ended and another bonded area was established in Régua, thus enabling small Douro farmers, who had meanwhile changed their status to that of producers-bottlers, to ship their wine directly from the Douro. Contrary to past regulations, farmers are no longer required to sell their wine to shippers only. Farmers can now sell part of their production to shippers, they can sell Port under their own label, and they can make table wine from the grapes that were not licensed for Port, all of which has become common practice.

The Douro region has a large surplus of grapes when compared to the needs of the Port trade. Of the 240,000 pipes of wine produced in the region, half, or in certain years, less than half, are made into Port. The surplus wine that in the past was handed over to the Casa do Douro to be distilled is currently made into table wine. Consequently, since the 50s the Douro, as is the case in other Portuguese winemaking regions, has seen a growth in the number of Co-operative Wineries; aside from Estremadura, the Douro is the region with the greatest number of such associations. In addition to producing table wine, these wineries also make Port that they sell under their own label.

With a view to accommodating the interests of farmers and merchants, the government recently created the Inter-professional Committee for the Demarcated Douro Region (CIRDD), an entity that has assumed some of the responsibilities that used to belong to the Casa do Douro. It is within the framework of this new organisational model that the region strives to resolve centuries-old conflicts and dissension between farmers and merchants. This is most likely the best way to reconcile the occasionally conflicting interests of the several operators in the Port trade.

AFTER THREE HUNDRED YEARS, WHAT?

What did three hundred years of history do to change the Douro wilderness and how does the present social structure mirror a history that, looking back, cannot be considered anything but successful?

There are two contradictory visual aspects to the country-side. The visitor is impressed by the dimension of the work that it required of generations of people who laboured to cultivate a land that initially appeared destined to be a waste-land of scrub and trees. As you examine the landscape, you will also see the changes in the ways by which vines were planted and the number of new vineyards that are a true sign of the region's vitality. Nevertheless, as you venture further into the valleys and up the hillsides, the new face of the banks of the Douro and its tributaries cannot conceal the feeling that time appears to have stood still. The human settlements, the buildings and the people do not mirror the prosperity of a product that is said to have been successful for three hundred years. You become very aware of the rural nature of the land, as you would imagine it to have been fifty or a hundred years ago. The farmers are elderly, there is a high rate of illiteracy, signs of prosperity are rare, the economic power of the people, although it does exist, is not apparent. Traditions remain what they have always been; the harsh-ness of the countryside has moulded the people of the Douro forever.

Three hundred years later, there continues to be a British community in Porto, a community that retains its very British codes of behaviour, builds schools for its children fashioned according to the British system of education, has its Factory House (the oldest existing institution of its nature and the only remaining one in Europe), and entertains in its typically Victorian English clubs. This community, to which, in some cases, belong the fifth generations of families that have always lived in Portugal, enjoys speaking Portuguese with an English accent and its members continue to hold British passports. Although several of the original British firms have either dis-appeared from the scene or been absorbed by large interna-tional wine and spirits corporations, there still are vestiges of the old British tradition in the families that, generation after generation, continue to follow the British way of life.

4. Soil, Climate and three Sub-regions ~ a Multicoloured Douro

When we speak of the Demarcated Douro Region we are speaking of 250,000 hectares of land. This vast land, with its enormous regional differences and multiple variations that almost give birth to microclimates, is divided into three distinctly different sub-regions: Lower Corgo, Upper Corgo and Upper Douro.

The natural boundaries of this immense region are the Marão and Montemuro mountains to the west and Barca d'Alva on the Spanish border to the east. Although it is more difficult to set the boundaries to the north and to the south quite so clearly as these vary greatly, altitude also represents a limitation because one is not authorised to make either Port or Douro table wine from grapes grown above 600 and 700 metres, respectively.

The Lower Corgo, the Upper Corgo and the Upper Douro.

The schistous soil typical of the region.

From a geological viewpoint, schist is the predominating rock. This is a surface rock formation that has excellent properties for viticulture. It holds water well, enables the roots to dig deep into the subsoil and resists erosion; it retains heat during the day and transmits it to the vine at night. The vast schistous countryside of the Douro is supplemented by granite outcrops in certain areas, namely in the Upper Douro, and some more fertile alluvial soil in the Lower Corgo. This geological formation is indispensable to the quality of Port that is produced in the region. Although the amount of wine produced is always small, it enables vines to live long and the quality of the must is very high indeed.

The Douro climate is best illustrated by a local saying that describes the weather as "nine months of winter and three months of hell". The winter cold that one suffers in the Douro is exactly proportional to the scorching summer heat that leaves you almost breathless. Such contrasting weather has a marked effect on the wines of the region and makes the vines behave in different ways according to where they are planted. Vineyards that face south and west always receive a great deal of sunlight and heat; north-facing vineyards enable the grapes to ripen more smoothly. The age of the vine is an important factor in such a harsh climate. Old vines, with extremely long roots find it much easier to survive a particularly hot summer as their roots dig deep into the subsoil to obtain some water.

In the Upper Douro, the vineyards are planted on less sloping land which makes it possible for much of their work to be mechanised. Although in the past this sub-region was almost inaccessible due to the lack of roads and transportation and its distance from Porto, the Upper Douro is attracting an increasing number of supporters and is the region of preference for much of the new planting that is being done.

THE LOWER CORGO

The principle reason for dividing the Douro into three sub-regions has to do with the natural conditions of the soil and the climate that you find in each. The Lower Corgo that goes from Mesão Frio to the west, to a little above Régua, to the east (as far as the mouth of the River Corgo) is, as you can see on the map, the area with the greatest number of vines. Of a total area of 45,000 hectares, approximately 13,779 are under vine (34% of the total for the Demarcated Region).

As it is closer to Porto, has better lines of communication, contains important urban centres such as Régua, Lamego or Mesão Frio, this region naturally was the first to attract the attention of the Gaia merchants and the first in which Port was produced.

A fertile region where the green of the landscape dominates the attention of the traveller, the Lower Corgo is an

Distribution of the area under vine in the three sub-regions		
	Area under vine	Number of farmers
Lower Corgo	13 779	15 801
Upper Corgo	18 316	16 690
Upper Douro	8 627	7 800
Total	**40 721**	**40 291**

Source: Casa do Douro

Socalcos - **earth - banked, terrassed vineyards.**

area of great productivity and of a greater rainfall that produces less concentrated and less complex wines. It is an
excellent region for table wine and for average quality Port.
Nevertheless, such a sweeping statement is a bit unfair as
it excludes the excellent wine that is now produced in the
region following the introduction of modern winemaking
techniques and the planting of new vineyards, and the
appearance of a previously practically non-existent attention
to quality. As you look at the countryside you will see, in
addition to vines, vegetables and groves of fruit trees such
as the olive, cherry, fig, orange and almond. The people of
this sub-region never cease to proclaim the virtues of their

vegetables, the excellence of their fruit and the quality of their wine.

Although the Lower Corgo is authorised to produce Port, none of its vineyards have been attributed the highest classification of A, which means that fewer vineyards are allocated a license to be made into Port than others of a similar size in the Upper Corgo or Upper Douro sub-regions.

THE UPPER CORGO

The Upper Corgo sub-region runs from the River Corgo valley to the west, up to the Valeira Gorge, to the east. It covers an area of 95,000 hectares, of which 18,316 are under vine (45% of the total in the Demarcated Region).

Here, the countryside changes quite noticeably as you leave the exuberantly green rolling hillsides of the Lower Corgo and enter deep, steep valleys where the land becomes more aggressive and the landscape is less tamed. You will occasionally see some Mediterranean shrubs and flora typical of dryer regions such as gum cistus, broom, bushmint and rosemary.

Vineyards in this region are always less lush then in the Lower Corgo and the soil is schistose and very stony. You get the sense that work in these vineyards is much more arduous; some especially steep and craggy hillsides may even lead you to wonder how such an inhospitable region could create one of the finest wines in the world.

The Upper Corgo is the doorway to the heart of the region from whence comes the majority of the great Port wines, within a 15 to 20 Km radius around the village of Pinhão, where you will find most of the quintas that produce superior quality Port. The secret to this quality resides in a set of factors, the main one being the union of the schistous soil and a more aggressive climate – very cold winters and burning hot summers. The vineyard suffers more, yield per vine is less but the quality is notably superior.

In this sub-region, the valleys of the tributaries to the River Douro are totally covered with vineyards and it is here where some of the greatest Port quintas, are located. In the Douro, the meaning of the Portuguese word *Quinta* is slightly different from the usual translation of "wine estate". Quinta means, above all, the vineyards; a Douro quinta is more than a country property with a vineyard on it. Some quintas have no buildings on them at all.

Here and there, you will see large wineries, some of them built according to the latest winemaking standards. Several of these wineries have been built from scratch over the past few years. The tendency today is especially for medium-sized wineries where large amounts of wine can be made but that can also produce small amounts of very special wine. You may also see a scattering of white balloon-shaped cement tanks that used to be used to store large amounts of wine.

Following the new plantings of the 80s that succeeded the introduction of the PDRITM (Plan for the Integrated Rural Development of the Trás-os-Montes), the vineyards in the Upper Corgo underwent major changes as the new planting had to obey a new set of criteria regarding the planting methods (inter-locking terraces, or *patamares*, and later, vertical terraces, or *vinhas ao alto*) and choice of the varieties of vines (planting of five select red wine varietals).

The Upper Douro

To a certain extent, the Upper Douro is both an innovation and a revelation. Bordered to the west by the Valeira Gorge and to the east by the Spanish frontier, the Upper Douro is an immense region covering 110,000 hectares, yet it has proportionately the least amount of land under vine in the entire Demarcated Douro Region – 8,627 hectares (21% of the total in the Demarcated Region).

When I speak of it as an innovation, I am thinking of the little importance that for so many years was attributed to this sub-region. With the exception of a few famous quintas such as Vesúvio or Vargellas, the Upper Douro never appeared to interest either farmers or shippers. The great distances that separated it from Porto and Gaia, together with the difficulties in transport and communication, were sufficient reasons for the lack of investment on their part.

Nevertheless, the Upper Douro has everything that could interest the investor. The vineyards here are easily mechanised, production costs are lower and the high quality of its wines remains pretty consistent year after year. Although this is the most arid land in the region, it still manages to produce superior quality wines, and here lies the revelation. Firms and farmers who are directing their efforts to this area and who are purchasing vineyards or making the wines from the Upper Douro separately from the others, today recognise the great potential this extensive sub-region has to offer. Furthermore, considering the little amount of authorised land that is currently under vine, you cannot say that it is because of a lack of suitable land for vineyards that the Douro might face difficulties in the future.

5. Vineyards and Vines
~ Past & Present

The history of the planting of the vineyards in the Douro is as magnificent as it is dramatic. When you look at the steep slopes, you can easily get an idea of the colossal amount of work that went into shaping the landscape.

The Douro region is not totally "unique" in this regard, as there are other winemaking regions, such as the Moselle in Germany, where man also laboured to sculpt the land and adapt it to the demands of viticulture. Yet the Douro is different. Not only is the amount of land under vine considerably more impressive, as the work of man is much more manifest.

Because of the rolling hillsides that characterise the topography of the region, the vineyards always had to be constructed according to the physical aspects of the land; even today the vineyards follow the curves of the hillsides as the land under vine blends with the rest of the countryside to form a harmonious landscape.

The soil of much of the Douro that is under vine is very rocky which not only makes it extremely difficult to care for the vines as it was difficult for the men who had to face the awesome task of building the terraces that support each vineyard. Awesome, not to say Herculean, when you consider that before the existence of the mechanical equipment, such as bulldozers and tractors, that farmers now use, all the work had to be done by hand – and it was, by thousands upon thousands of workers.

There are two great epochs in the history of the vineyard – the period before and the one that followed the phylloxera. As vineyards were abandoned following the destruction caused by the phylloxera, man was forced to try the other planting methods that I described earlier.

A terrassed vineyard.

There are three different types of traditional vineyards: very narrow, pre-phylloxera terraces, or *socalcos*, and two types of post-phylloxera terraces whose width varied according to the slope of the land. With gradients of up to 30%, where the accentuated slope sometimes only allowed for a single row of vines, the sides of the socalcos were buttressed by dry stone walls that accompanied the curve of the land. The stone for the walls was obtained either from broken pieces of schist as the land was scarified or from the bits of rock that broke off when dynamite was used to break up larger blocks of stone. Before mechanisation invaded the Douro, all this was done by hand, with the assistance of tools such as pick axes, crowbars and hoes and much of the labour necessary to build these hundreds of kilometres of walls came from Galicia in northern Spain or from outlying villages.

These narrow terraces were the hallmark of the Douro land-scape for over two centuries. Today, the many that remain are almost considered as monuments. There even is a government grant for farmers who of their own free will wish to rebuild the walls that have crumbled over the years. The purpose of this grant is to preserve of one of the most distinct charac-teristics of the Douro valley and the most poignant (not to say distressing) memorial to the immense task of transforming an inhospitable land into a winemaking region.

All the construction work on these walls began from bottom to top, always accompanying the curve and the level of the land. Beginning at the very bottom, at the lower altitude the men worked their way up as far as they could go and still plant vines. This is why some hillsides are totally covered with vines. With this system, the correct amount of water was retained in the soil whilst the natural permeability of the walls kept it from becoming waterlogged.

Several changes were made to this method for constructing a vineyard after the phylloxera as many vineyards were abandoned and the land was never again used to plant vines. As time passed and the terraces were no longer tended, supporting walls began to crumble and the socalcos generated into the wastelands of today. In the Douro, they are known as mortuaries for their smell of death, of Man's despair and his desertion of the land. The visitor is overwhelmed by the great number of *mortórios* that litter the countryside witness to the social and human devastation caused by this microscopic insect's subterranean activities.

No further radical changes were to be made to the surface landscape. Gradually, mortórios were planted with groves of olive and almond trees and where this has not occurred, shrubs and the wild vegetation typical of a Mediterranean climate have overrun the abandoned terraces.

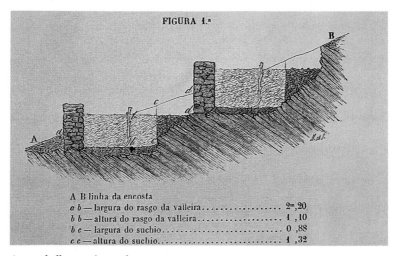

FIGURA 1.ª

A B linha da encosta
a b — largura do rasgo da valleira.................. 2m,20
b b — altura do rasgo da valleira.................... 1 ,10
b c — largura do suchio........................... 0 ,88
c c — altura do suchio............................ 1 ,32

A pre-phylloxera vineyard.

An ancient vineyard.

The main viticultural change to the vineyard as a result of the phylloxera was the introduction of American rootstock. Since then, these vines whose roots appear immune to the phylloxera, have become indispensable to farmers and a new skill has been introduced in the treatment of the vineyard: grafting. The farmer begins by planting the rootstock and the following year he grafts the vine that he has previously selected onto this rootstock. Many farmers today prefer to plant the so-called ready-made grafted vines: these are cuttings of selected vine varieties that are sent to specialist growers who cultivate the rootstock, graft the cuttings and return them ready for planting in the vineyard. Although this new practice offers the added advantage of guaranteeing the quality of the rootstock and their immunity to disease, there are still many farmers who prefer not to adopt this method as, contrary to that which they originally expected, in practice, it does not actually save them that one year during the infancy of the vine.

The planting methods that were introduced after the phylloxera made it possible for five and six rows of vines to be planted on each terrace, a practice that almost doubled the number of vines per hectare; from 3,500 vines per hectare, farmers now planted approximately 6,000 vines. The walls no longer followed the curve of the land quite so precisely and their overall appearance was more geometric. This new system not only reduced the amount of manpower that was required as fewer walls had to be built, as it improved the yield per hectare.

These planting techniques survived mostly unchanged until the 1970s when, due to the lack of manpower and the sharp rises in the cost of labour that made mechanisation of the vineyard an imperative, that farmers were forced to resort to other planting methods.

The socalcos were gradually replaced by *patamares*, wide inter-locking terraces supported by banks of earth. Built on identical principles, these new terraces no longer required buttressing with dry stone walls and, most importantly, could

Grafting.

be easily mechanised. The height of the banks of earth varies according to the slope of the land and some may be as much as 5 metres tall. The vineyards are now scarified from top to bottom, special attention being made to the drainage of the land so as to avoid landslides during heavy downpours of rain and to giving due access to tractors and other machines.

In spite of the fact that this system makes mechanisation possible, there are several disadvantages to it: there is some unequal growth of the vines that are now planted in several rows, spraying of the row of vines closest to the edge of the terrace is difficult, the profuse growth of weeds and wild grasses on the banks adds work and resort to undesirable herbicides.

In the 1980s, a totally new system based on a German method was introduced in an attempt to overcome these problems. This is the method by which the vineyards are built along the steepest slope of the land, a technique known as *vinha ao alto*, or vertical vineyard. Mechanisation is now total and initial concerns that such a method would not prove viable have been discarded. This is the system of the future that little by little is transforming the Douro landscape. It does have its limitations, principally that it cannot be used on land where the gradient exceeds 40% as this would not be safe for machines and would make the tasks that still have to be performed by hand, such as picking the grapes at the vintage, extremely difficult.

There are some major vineyards in the region where the several methods can be found side by side; this is the 1990s version of the Douro mosaic.

VINES AND THEIR VARIETALS
– A COMPLEX UNIVERSE

Every country surrounding the Mediterranean Sea that has a centuries-old winemaking tradition boasts a wide range of types of vines that it uses to make wine. It is therefore not surprising that numerous types of vines proliferate in every winemaking region in Portugal. The Douro is no exception to this with almost a hundred recognised varietals. Obviously, there are extreme variations in the quality of the product and one can even say that the majority are of only passing interest for winemaking purposes. Twenty-nine grapevines (15 red and 14 white) are currently recommended for wines that will bear the Port Denomination of Origin.

Although farmers have always known how to distinguish between good and bad vines, the present day concept of a superior quality varietal may be very different from that of the past. In the old days, vines that produced a very high yield were considered a blessing; these were the so-called "debt-paying vines" given their extreme generosity. At a time when there was little scientific oenology, a variety that proved resistant to diseases of the vine was also considered extremely valuable.

We now know that some varieties that farmers thought little of were disparaged due to no fault of their own: lacking the scientific knowledge of today, they had no other choice than refuse varieties that produced few grapes or were especially subject to disease. The case of the **Touriga Nacional** is perhaps the best example of this. For many, many years, this vine was considered undesirable for precisely those reasons. The fact of the matter is that this vine had been poorly studied from the oenological aspect. By poorly studied I mean that farmers did not know which rootstock would best adapt itself to the specific characteristics of the Douro, the best way to train the vines, the best distance between plants and the best vine density per hectare, or the best care to be given the vine throughout its growing cycle, i.e., how to best lop the leaves: which leaves should be left on the vine and which should be removed so as to control the amount of sunlight the bunches of grapes would receive.

Scholars of the Douro, writing as far back as the 16th century, refer to the vine varieties in the region. Several 18th century authors were also interested in this subject but their opinions as to the validity of these vines were inevitably greatly empirical. You must also not forget that the way that these vines performed before the advent of the phylloxera was quite different from their present day behaviour. The fact is that as the pre-phylloxera vines were planted directly into the soil, they produced wines that were much deeper in colour. This explains why some vine varieties that are poorly thought of today, such as Mourisco or Tinta Francisca, were highly recommended then.

Much of the more recent research on Douro varietals was carried out at the end of the 70s and 80s by José Rosas and João Nicolau de Almeida who spent five years studying the vines and comparing statistical data. Consequently, in the 1980s when farmers were authorised to significantly increase the area of their land under vine, there was a consensus as to which were the best varietals that should be planted.

Port is always the end product of a blend of several varieties. This is nothing new as, roughly speaking, it is line with the traditional practice in other "old" European winemaking countries. It has always been accepted that the complexity that a winemaker can obtain in a wine made from a blend of several varieties is much superior to that which he can obtain in a wine made from a single varietal. The reason is simple: a single varietal rarely contains high levels of all the factors that are required of a perfect wine. For example, a great red wine (either Port or table wine) must be endowed with intense colour and a rich aroma, be full-bodied, have the correct acidity to ensure its vigour, must contain delicate tannins and present an elegant finish. This is a lot to ask for from a single vine. By blending several varietals it is much easier as some contain a great deal of colour but little aroma, others are full of quality aromas but are not very full-bodied, etc.

Until very recently, the complementarity of the varietals was decided upon in the vineyard and not in the winery. The vineyards were planted with rows of different vines, sometimes dozens of different varieties in a same vineyard. For what reason? When the grapes were picked, some would not be fully ripe and thus would contribute with a greater acidity to the wine; other grapes that were excessively ripe would provide body and structure; others would give it colour but little aroma, and so on. This concept of creating the blend in the vineyard is still advocated by some in the Port trade although it has been clearly established that better results can be obtained otherwise.

The Douro suffers an added disadvantage: the enormity of the region and the consequent diversity of soils and micro climates mean that a same vine will behave differently according to where it is planted. A vine planted in the Lower Corgo will definitely produce different results than if it is planted in the Upper Douro. Recent studies have been directed at adapting the varieties of vines to the location and

The vintage.

to the specific microclimate. Experimental plantings have been made in the three sub-regions and micro vinification has been carried out for each varietal in each region. It has thus been possible to determine, with a great degree of precision, the best combination of varietal, soil, location and specific microclimate for each region. It is this unique combination of factors that produces a wine of unequalled quality, what the French call *terroir*, an expression that applies without reservation to the Douro.

All new plantings take the complementarity of the different vines into account, but these are planted in separate plots and each varietal is duly separated from the other. In this case, the role of the winemaker is to determine exactly just what he wants to obtain from the grapes and when, according to the type of wine he desires to make. First, he makes the different wines, then his blend.

There have been several experiments in making a single varietal Port but the result has always been inferior to the one obtained from a blend of selected varieties. The new plantings have confirmed that Touriga Nacional, when it is well worked from an oenological viewpoint, is a truly excellent vine. Although still in the early stages, its presence on the Douro hillsides is increasing. All new plantings include some of this varietal, considered by many as the best Portuguese red grapevine.

CHOOSING THE BEST VARIETIES

As a result of the research, five red varieties were selected and recommended for the 2,500 hectares of land that were to be newly planted under the scope of the PDRITM. It was concluded that a balanced lot of wine would contain the complementary characteristics of five different varietals: Touriga Nacional, Tinto Cão, Tinta Barroca, Tinta Roriz and Touriga Francesa. All the five are not always included in each lot of wine. Several combinations are possible, with percentages varying from one lot to another, particularly as the extreme variation in microclimates produce wines that are not always the same, even when the varietal is the same. In the

An Autumn landscape.

end, it is up to each winemaker is to determine which the best blend of the several wines that he has to work with.

Each of the above five varietals has very different characteristics, yet between them they create a very well balanced wine. Let us compare two of these, **Touriga Nacional** and **Tinta Roriz**. Touriga is not very farmer-friendly as it usually yields less than a Kilogram of grapes per vine although this may be as high as 1.5 Kgs; Roriz, on the other hand, produces almost 2.5 Kgs of grapes per vine. Naturally, a must obtained from Touriga is much more concentrated than one made from Roriz.

This latter varietal, **Tinta Roriz**, is the only one that is widely planted outside Portugal, mainly in Spain where it contributes greatly to the wines made in the Rioja and the Ribera del Duero regions where it is called Tempranillo and elsewhere in Spain, Tinto Fino or Cencibel. This vine appears to have been brought to Portugal from Spain (references to this date back to 1800) when it was first planted in the south under the name of Tinta Aragonesa or Aragonês, especially in the Alentejo where it is one of the principal red varieties.

The men of the Douro jokingly refer to it as a vine that "is very good, when it feels like it!" Another expression frequently used is that some varieties, such as Roriz, are very "yearly"; in the sense that their quality varies from year to year, some good and some bad.

Roriz is considered suitable for all kinds of wine: when the vine is allowed to produce an excessive number of bunches of grapes, it is good for making a rosé; when its production is controlled, it makes a good backup wine. It does not perform equally well on all types of soils, as it is sensitive to any lack in minerals in the soil in which it is planted. Roriz today represents some 12% of all grafted varieties in the region and, in the case of Port, is considered as a good blending wine, although it needs to be complemented with other wines in order to obtain good results.

As regards table wine, Tinta Roriz is already used in significant amounts in Portugal. Some excellent wines have been made from these grapes not just in the Douro and the Dão but also in the Alentejo, which just goes to prove that when well made, this varietal can produce a great wine.

Touriga Nacional is the variety most revered by farmers today, not just in the Douro but in other winemaking regions as well. It has become a sort of Portuguese Cabernet as, likewise to the French vine, it adapts itself well to several types of soil and climate. In addition to the Douro and the Dão where this vine was born and became famous, Touriga is spreading to all of Portugal; it is becoming known worldwide and has already arrived in Australia.

Thanks to recent viticultural advances, Touriga no longer suffers the stigma of being a low-yield vine that led farmers to belittle it in the past. The concept of complexity is fully expressed with the Touriga: fruity aroma, good in the mouth and full-bodied, an elegant and distinguished finish. Without a doubt, this is a great varietal. Its virtues are reflected in the several types of table wine made from Touriga that have recently appeared on the Portuguese market, a trend that is expected to grow in importance over the next few years.

In the case of Port there is an added difficulty that does not apply to table wine in that good Port is made to last for many years, either in bottle or in wood. Especially because of this, the winemaker must know which varieties will confer good qualities to the wine over long periods of time. The problem resides, for example, in that a good aroma when a wine is young may, after twenty years in bottle, go awry. Hence, a winemaker needs to constantly balance that which is introduced through new technologies and the age-old knowledge and skills that have been handed down over the years. It is this knowledge that enables him to judge just how a specific aroma in a young wine will smell 20 years later. When a winemaker tastes young wines he must bear in mind that he is not blending lots that will be drunk the following year but instead that he is making a wine whose personality should stand up to the test of time.

Tinto Cão is a perfect illustration of what I have just said: as some of its virtues will only become apparent as it develop and ages, this variety must be included when making up lots that are expected to age for many years.

One of the five chosen Douro varieties, this is the one that has the least amount of colour and the greatest tendency to oxidise and, although its qualities will only develop over time, the winemaker must be prepared for this initial lack of appeal. Even in the case of table wine, this variety is always better when blended with other varieties. Several producers have been experimenting with making a table wine solely from Tinto Cão; the results have always proved to be more "feminine" than robust. This femininity has also been widely noted in the Dão where such wines are also being made.

The most representative vine in Douro vineyards (approximately 22% of all plantings) is **Touriga Francesa**. Its name is extremely misleading as this vine has no relation whatsoever to any known French vine; quite the contrary, it is a typical Douro variety. This variety, when examined on its own, has little to recommend it from a purely oenological viewpoint. It does, however, have a very characteristic bouquet that enriches any lot of wine with which it is blended. Furthermore, it has other, no less interesting, advantages: yield is quite consistent – approximately 2.5 Kg per vine – and it adapts itself well to several different types of soil. As its grapes are highly resistant to extreme heat thanks to their thick skin, it is planted widely in the Upper Douro. It does, however, require some winemaking care as it tends to

oxidise easily and therefore lose the floral aromas for which it is known. It also has the additional advantage in that it can be used both for table and for Port wine.

So far, there have been no extensive experiments to determine Touriga Francesa's capabilities as a single variety table wine. Not very well known outside the Douro, in recent studies this vine has proven to adapt itself well to the sandy soil of the Setubal region and as such may be of future interest.

After Touriga Francesa and Tinta Roriz, the next most frequently planted vine in the Douro (11.6% of all vines) is **Tinta Barroca**. This is a very ancient varietal as early references to it date back to the 17th century. Like other Douro varieties, Tinta Barroca has already travelled beyond the Portuguese frontier and is currently being used, albeit more as a curiosity, in some South African table wines. It gives a good yield, approximately 2.5 Kg per vine, and is one of the earliest to be harvested as it can rapidly become over-ripe and produce a thick wine that needs to be complemented with wine from other varieties.

Wines that are made from the Tinta Barroca are always soft and full bodied, with aromas that differ according to whether it is planted in a cooler or in a sunnier vineyard. When the grapes are picked at the ideal moment, the wine usually contains very high levels of sugar and a tremendous depth of colour that last very well when it is aged in bottle, one of the reasons it is usually included in a Vintage Port. Contrary to Touriga Francesa, the skins of the grapes are very thin and these can easily become raisins, which is why the farmer must choose the exact moment to pick them else they become unsuitable for Vintage. Furthermore, excessive ripeness may lead to the appearance of acetic bacteria that would also rule it out for this purpose. This vine is very well known in the Lower and the Upper Corgo; in the Upper Douro where it is usually harvested two to three weeks earlier than other varieties, it demands a great deal of care and attention.

The very few experiments in producing a single variety table wine with these grapes have not yet indicated any special characteristics of note nor has its true value yet been determined.

In addition to the five most noble varieties of vines, there are others that are profusely planted in the Douro. The most important of these is **Tinta Amarela**, often found in the Lower Corgo and also widely planted in other Portuguese winemaking regions such as Ribatejo, Estremadura and Alentejo where it is known under the name of Trincadeira Preta. This variety represents about 7% of all vines planted but in the Douro it still suffers great problems as the vine is extremely prone to disease and its grapes, to rot, which is why it was not included in the list of the top varieties. Tinta Carvalha, Bastardo, Sousão, Alvarelhão, Tinta Francisca and Mourisco are also planted in the Douro and may, in the future, become more widely used when oenologists find a way to overcome one their most marked disadvantages, namely their very low yield which makes them quite unprofitable for the moment.

White grape varieties for Port and table wine

To the consumer, the words Douro and Port are synonymous with red wine. Nevertheless, white grape varieties still occupy their fair share of the vineyards in the region – more precisely 34% of all plantings – quite a fair amount.

From the moment when white grapes ceased to be mixed with the red grapes that were being made into wine, they became available for a wide range of uses. In addition to White Port, a relative recent invention that boasts no great tradition in the history of the Douro, the region also produces a white table wine and a Moscatel, particularly in the area of Alijó and Favaios.

The Douro's harsh and hot climate is perhaps not best suited for white wines that are best made where summers are not quite so scorching and the weather is more so that the grapes can ripen more evenly. None of this happens at lower altitudes in the Douro and this is why white vines are usually planted higher up the hillsides, where it is cooler. There where a vineyard is too high for it to be attributed a Port license, white grapevines are planted for table wine. When white grapes are destined for Port, the vines are planted in more traditional but in cooler, less sunny areas.

Some authors suggest that only two varieties of vines present any characteristics of note: Moscatel and Malvasia Fina. The latter of the two is widely planted in other Portuguese winemaking regions but under another name.

You have to distinguish clearly between the varieties that are best for table wine and those used for Port. The enormous oenological requirements for a good white table wine cannot be compared to the greater ease with which a winemaker can produce a good White Port from these grapes.

White Port has always been considered to be a lesser off-shoot of the Port trade. Often quite rightly so but not, in my opinion, always fairly. A good old White Port that, curiously, over the years may have acquired the style of an old tawny, can also be a magnificent wine that will afford a great deal of pleasure. The fact of the matter is that this type of White Port is rare and expensive and most consumers are not prepared to pay as much for an old White Port as they are for an old Tawny Port that is made from red grapes.

Furthermore, winemakers do not appear to be as concerned with the proportion of the different white varieties that are used in making up a lot of White Port, which is why it is always more difficult to describe the idiosyncrasies of this type of wine.

In addition to **Malvasia Fina** that produces wines with a delicate aroma, there are other varieties. **Códega** is a very ancient Portuguese varietal and is highly regarded by farmers for two major reasons: yields are very high and its wines have a very high degree of alcohol. As these wines tends to be low in acidity, they need to be complemented with a wine that will give them some verve.

Malvasia Real is another varietal from the great family of the Malvasia vines but it is of less interest than the above as although its yield is high, the resulting wine is neither very rich nor complex.

Rabigato, Gouveio, Viosinho and Arinto are other varieties planted in the region. Normally, when made as a single variety wine they have little personality of their own but, particularly in the case of table wine, may produce some "uncommon" wines, in the sense that they are different from the ones most often produced

Arriving in the winery.

to suit the taste of present-day consumers. The current, somewhat excessive preoccupation in making very fruity light wines may lead the consumer to forget that there are other good quality products that deserve to be known. The Douro will never be able to compete with other regions in producing light fruity wines because its climate is not suitable for this. In can, however, produce several different types of white wine, but always in very reduced amounts.

As to White Port, it appears to me that producers are not really seriously investing in changing existing styles. White Port shall continue to be a delightful aperitif wine, served chilled and accompanied by some freshly toasted Douro almonds or, even better, a fine *paté de foie gras*. I don't really see how it could be turned into a wine that you would drink at the end of a meal.

REGISTRY OF VINEYARDS AND THE "BENEFÍCIO"

From the early days when the Douro region was demarcated, farmers had a clear idea of the varying quality of the wine and of the fact that this quality depended on where the vineyards were located. As we saw earlier, the government then took care to create a register containing the classification of all the vineyards and, consequently, the wines they produced as well.

When the Casa do Douro was established in 1932, one of its first tasks was precisely to create this register and to classify each and every plot of land under vine. This was a gigantic job considering that it involved some 30,000 farmers, 100,000 vineyards and two hundred million vines!

This registry was fundamental, as without it there could be no clear idea of each vineyard's potential to produce fortified wine. Depending on the quality of the vines, each vineyard was allotted a given amount of must that could be made into Port or, to use the Portuguese expression, to "benefit" the wine by adding brandy, thus transforming it into Port.

This apportionment became known as the *benefício* and the value of each vineyard and each quinta depended on the amount of benefício it was granted. Even today, quintas continue to be valued more according to their benefício than other more commonplace factors, as we see in other parts of the country. In the Douro, it really matters little whether the property includes a house or whether existing buildings are in good condition or not, the existence of a winery may be of little import, it doesn't really matter whether the property is walled in, whether it contains woodlands or fruit trees. The only factor that is consistently taken into account is the amount of the benefício. *Benefício* is the magic word that separates the good quintas from the bad. A quinta allotted many pipes of benefício is worth a small fortune.

The system under which the benefício is allotted is attributed to Álvaro Moreira da Fonseca and his work "Method for Apportioning the Benefício in the Douro Region". From then on each plot of land under vine was classified and allocate its respective license to make Port. Before this system was implemented, there was no limit to the amount of must that could be fortified nor was there a means to evaluate the value of the best musts. The annual amount of must that was fortified bore no relation to the demands of the market, which was not conducive to the balance of trade. The vineyards had to be recorded and classified in order to control production.

Once every factor is taken into account, a vineyard is classified from A to F, in descending order. Class A vineyards, being the best, are allotted the greatest amount of benefício;

Vintage.

F vineyards, being the least good for Port, are only permitted to fortify a small amount of must.

For each vineyard in the Douro to be classified according to this system, technical staff have to visit each vineyard and attribute a score to each of twelve separate parameters that are grouped under the general categories of **soil, climate** and **viticultural conditions**. The vineyard is then classified according to the total score obtained by all twelve parameters.

The two parameters that carry the most relative weight as regards the total score are productivity and altitude (21% each).

Productivity is decisive to the final product as it is felt that a vineyard with a very high yield will produce less concentrated musts and these are of less interest to Port. According to its yield per hectare, a vineyard will be given a score ranging from 0 (yields of 50 to 55 hectolitres/hectare) to +120 (yields of up to 36 hectolitres/hectare).

Altitude attributes more importance to the lower-lying vineyards (those closer to the level of the river) and penalises those located at higher altitudes. Altitude scores range from –900 (vineyards above an altitude of 650 m) to +240 (Upper Corgo and Upper Douro vineyards located between the level of the river – altitude 0 – and a maximum altitude of 150 m).

These are then followed, in decreasing importance, by the **nature of the land, location, viticultural conditions,** variety of vine, exposure and slope of the land. Of least importance to the final score are the planting density, rockiness of the soil, shelter and age of the vineyard.

The final classification is attributed on the basis of the total of all the twelve scores and there is no single scale. Let's take an example: in terms of productivity, a vineyard will score from 0 (extremely high yield per hectare) to +120 (very low yield); as regards the varieties of vines, it will score from -150 (varieties considered to be least good) to +150 (recommended varieties); as to height, its score will range between –900 and +150 according to the altitude at which it is planted.

Nature of the land refers to the type of soil in which the vineyard is planted. Schist has always been a hallmark of the land from which the finest Port is produced. Thus, this type of soil is most highly scored (+100), followed by soil that is in transition (-100), granite (-250) and alluvial (-400).

Location of the vineyard is another important parameter. For this purpose, the region is divided into 5 climatic zones

Parameters for evaluating vineyards - Casa do Douro 99.05.27		
Criteria	Minimum score	Maximum score
Soil and Climate		
Location	-50	600
Altitude	-900	240
Slope	1	101
Substratum *nature of the land*	-400	100
Gross elements *gravel*	0	80
Exposure	-30	100
Protection	0	60
Viticultural		
Yield *productivity*	-	120
Vines *varietals*	-300	150
Planting density	-	50
Training of vines *system*	-	100
Age of vineyard	0	60

separated by each other by imaginary vertical lines. Essentially, this parameter considers factors related to the weather (rainfall and temperature) as one goes from west to east, that is, from the Lower Corgo to the Upper Douro. This score ranges from 0 to +460.

Viticultural conditions refers to the way the vines themselves are planted and cultivated and the techniques used for training the vines. Lower growing vines obtain a higher score and taller plants, a lower score. There are adjustments that have to be made here, however, as there have been changes in the methods for training the vines and in the planting density, particularly following the recent introduction of vertical vineyards. This score ranges from –500 to +100.

In my opinion, **Variety of the vine** has not been given sufficient importance in the overall classification as it is only given a weight of 6.1% of the total score, which appears to be manifestly little. Traditionally, in the Douro, little importance was given to the factor vine variety yet all the new

planting points to a quite careful selection of varieties; farmers who are concentrating on these good varietals are not
been rewarded for their efforts in terms of their total scores.
For classification purposes, the vines are divided into five
groups: very good, good, average, mediocre and bad, with
scores ranging from +150 for the best to –300 for the worst.

Some farmers do not agree with the need to give greater
importance to the varieties of the vine. In their opinion, location, productivity and the age of the vineyard are greater
determiners of the final quality of the product. I personally
believe that sporadic comparative studies ought to be made
of the wines produced from the traditional vineyards against
those from the currently recommended varieties, so as to
obtain a clearer opinion of the matter. The theoretical supe-
riority of a vineyard simply does not exist. It is only by comparing the product – the wine – that one can obtain an idea
of its quality.

The list of recommended vines indicates 15 red and 14
white varieties that should be used for making Port. This
number is naturally tending to decrease and, as I said earlier,
recent studies now point to a group of only 5 varieties.

Exposure and **Slope of the land** are parameters beyond
the farmer's control. The vineyard is what it is and one cannot alter either its exposure or the natural slope of the land.
Vineyards planted on steeper slopes are more exposed to
the sun and are thus more highly scored, whereas flat vineyards are scored 0. A score of +101 is given to the steepest
(35%) land. As to exposure, south-facing vineyards obtain
the highest scores as they receive the most sunlight, thereby
enabling the grapes to ripen more fully. There is a lot of discussion between farmers regarding this latter parameter, as
north-facing vineyards occasionally fare better during particularly hot dry summers as they are less exposed to the sun
and the grapes ripen more evenly. This is, however, the exception to a rule that applies equally worldwide: grapes grown
on hillsides that are more exposed to the sun tend to be riper
and have a greater potential to produce a quality wine.

Once all the scores are added up, the vineyard is classified
according to the following scale:

Classification of Vineyards According to Total Score	
A	more than 1200 points
B	1001 to 1200 points
C	801 to 1000 points
D	601 to 800 points
E	401 to 600 points
F	201 to 400 points

ALLOCATION OF THE BENEFÍCIO

The amount of benefício – expressed in pipes of wine – is allocated to each vineyard as a function of the total score it has obtained on all twelve parameters. Vineyards with the highest scores will be authorised to produce more Port; those with the lowest scores, will be allocated little benefício. Each farmer is issued a "benefício card" indicating the amount of pipes of must he is authorised to make into Port. In the Douro, this document is worth more than its weight in gold and is an object that is often transacted amongst farmers.

The government did foresee the possibility that a small farmer who does not have the facilities for making his grapes into wine may wish to sell his benefício together with his grapes. The card, thus, acts as a form of printed currency as it is worth (or is potentially worth) a great deal of money. Theoretically, this can be highly advantageous to the purchaser. Let's look at a practical example. A farmer's vineyard is well located, on land classified either A or B, but the amount of benefício he has been allocated is insufficient to cover all his grapes, which means that some of them will be made into Port and the rest into table wine. In this case, when he purchases a benefício card he is actually buying the possibility of making all his grapes into Port. So far, so good.

The problems arise when a card is sold without the respective grapes, which subverts the entire logic on which the system is based. As long as the card system exists, these will continue to be sold and only a constant updating of the vineyard registry will help avoid greater evils.

All winemaking regions that are subject to very strict regulations are subject to system failures. It is not just the sale of these cards that interferes with the system that is applied in the Douro. There are forms of fraud such as bringing grapes into the Douro from outside the region or using concentrated must – a technique that raises the alcohol content of the musts and increases production–without the express authorisation of the supervisory entities, that the authorities are actively combating.

The total annual amount of must that is licensed as benefício varies and is established each year by the trade and the farmers' representatives, under the CIRDD (Interprofessional Committee for the Douro Demarcated Region), the entity responsible for publishing the annual "vintage manifesto" before the beginning of the harvest.

The concept of an annual restriction in the amount of Port that may be produced each year is applauded by most and disputed by a few. At heart, in the opinion of those who defend this limitation, is the attempt to balance the production of Port and thereby avoid creating a supply greatly in excess of the demand for this wine. Determination, by administrative order, of the amount of must that may be made into Port forces a balance between the amount of wine that is licensed and existing stocks, sales the previous year and the expected production for each year. This is the only way that one can ensure that the market is not flooded with Port, which would create situations of rupture and allow prices to get out of control.

Those who oppose the benefício system argue that it makes no sense for the amount of wine denominated Port to be attributed before a harvest by means of a vintage manifesto. The benefício is criticised on the basis that it is apportioned before one knows whether the grapes will superior quality or less healthy. Their suggestion is that the Denomination of Port should be attributed as a function of the quality of the wine and not by means of a simple administrative measure that is published before the wine itself is made. The system as it stands, they say, may lead to situations whereby in bad years (such as 1988, where the weather was most unfavourable to the vegetative cycle of the grape) the amount of benefício that is allocated may be greater then the amount of actual grapes produced, a situation that could favour more shady business practices.

I see no signs of any form of explicit desire to change the benefício system. Even though it is far from perfect, this system has managed to sustain a balance between the offer and demand for Port; furthermore, over the past few years, exports have been continuously on the rise.

THE LAW OF THE ONE THIRD

From the moment that the Companhia was created in 1756 to this day, the Douro has been unceasingly subject to control by laws, rules, regulations and restrictions to the activities of Port farmers and merchants. History has proven the justice of some and the trade has taken care to get rid of many others. The "Douro issue" is a recurring topic in the electoral manifestos of parties belonging to every shade of the political rainbow and it is not unusual for two persons to fight side by side in support of an issue which, under different circumstances, would find them on opposite sides of the fence.

One of the innovations introduced to the region under the Salazar regime was the so-called law of the one third. According to this law, which is still in force, each year shippers are only authorised to sell a maximum amount equivalent to one third of their total stock of Port. If you bear in mind that, for a Port firm to be created it must have a minimum stock of 300 pipes of wine, you will understand why so few new firms have appeared on the scene this century.

The underlying concept is that by forcing shippers to build up their stock they will be forced to age their wines. In the event that a shipper wishes to sell more wine than the one third that he is authorised to sell under law (the so-called sales capacity), his only alternative is to buy wine from farmers. The spirit of the law is that no one should increase in size without assisting others to do the same: a firm's business may grow and in doing so, so will the affairs of the farmers with whom it has to negotiate.

6. Making Port Wine
~ A Many Faceted Art

Port cannot be made without two inseparable elements: wine and grape spirit. It is the process of adding grape spirit, better known as brandy, to a must that enables a winemaker to take an ordinary wine and transform it into Port. Let's first take a look at how the wine is made and then we'll talk about the brandy.

Before the grapes are transported to the winery, they must be picked. In the Douro, the history of the grape harvest, or vintage, is a long and arduous one, abundant in sacrifices but also in moments of great happiness.

The entire calendar in the Douro revolves around the vintage. This is the time of the year when farmers harvest the

VITICULTURA E VINICULTURA

The *roga*.
Harvesting the grapes
the old-fashioned way.

fruit of a year's labour and it is always a period of great uncertainty as no one can predict what the weather might be hiding up its sleeve. That this uncertainly lasts until the very last day of the harvest is confirmed by a popular saying that goes like this: "the vintage is not over until the last basket has been washed and stored".

The Douro has always been sparsely settled and consequently has suffered, and continues to suffer, from a grave lack of manpower that is particularly acute at the time of the harvest when vast numbers of workers are needed in the vineyards and the wineries. The vintage lasts several weeks and, as all houses pick their grapes and make their wine almost simultaneously, labour has to be brought in from outside. This is the origin of the *rogas*, the groups of itinerant workers who travel to the Douro from the neighbouring provinces of Beiras, Trás-os-Montes and even further afield. A roga is a group of a couple of dozen men, women and a few teenagers, often from the same village and same families, contracted to work under a same foreman for the same farmer, generation after generation.

The members of the roga divide the work amongst themselves: women pick the grapes and place them in baskets and the young persons and men carry them to the pickup points from where they are taken to the winery. Although in the past large wicker baskets containing 60 Kgs of grapes were used, today they have been mostly replaced by 20-Kg containers. In the old days, the baskets were carried on men's backs down to the winery or onto an ox cart; today, they are simply loaded upon tractors. Picking of the grapes normally lasts some 10 to 12 hours a day, usually under a blazing sun. The day's work does not finish here as there is still much left to do later, in the treading tank, or *lagar*.

THE "LAGAR" – THE TRADITIONAL METHOD FOR MAKING PORT

The word *Lagar* has two meanings in the Douro: on the one hand it is used to describe the granite tanks where grapes are trod and the juice ferments; on the other hand, it is often used to mean the winery as a whole. To say that one "is taking

the grapes to the lagar" may mean to unload the grapes directly into the stone treading tanks or just to deliver the grapes to the winery.

With the traditional method, the grapes are tipped into the treading tank as they arrive at the winery. Made of large blocks of granite, a lagar is a very large, square or rectangular, tank with 80-cm high side walls. The capacity of each lagar varies greatly but each usually contains about fifteen pipes, that is, approximately 7,500 litres of wine. There are smaller (about 5,000 litres) and larger (up to 20,000 litres) lagares. The floor of the lagar is made of the same granite blocks. Although schist is the predominant rock formation in the Douro, its lack of compactness and hardness makes it improper for this purpose. Granite offers all the necessary characteristics for treading grapes and for fermenting a must. Another reason for its use throughout the region is that it is much easier to clean.

Lagares were usually built against one of the outside walls of the winery, under a window, so that the grapes could be tipped directly into the tank from outside the building as they arrived at the winery. Occasionally in the past, a circular winepress was placed in the centre of a lagar to press the skins that were behind after the grapes had been trod and the new wine had been removed.

A lagar should be filled only with the grapes picked that day so as to stop them from beginning to ferment before the time is right. The lagar work begins in the evening, once the picking for that day is over. There are several distinctly different stages to this work.

A lagar is only considered full when the grapes reach a distance of 25 cm from its top edge. As we shall see later, it must not be too full. Before treading begins, however, a small amount of sulphurous acid is added to the grapes to prevent the growth of acetic bacteria that could turn the must into vinegar.

The first step in the treading is the so-called *corte*, that is, when a group of men – two for every 750 Kgs of grapes – their arms closely linked together to form two facing rows, move slowly back and forth across the lagar for the first cut, or crushing, of the grapes. With great solemnity, at a slow and steady rhythm, the men simultaneously raise first one foot then another from the bottom of the tank and then bring it down again, each time crushing more grapes and gradually separating the juice from the skins and the stems. Left, right, left, right. In total silence, under the watchful eye of the foreman. This operation lasts about two hours and can be very painful as the stalks scratch and scrape at the workers' feet and legs. The synchronised movement ensures that all the grapes but none of the pips are evenly crushed.

Crushing the grapes in the lagar.

Several firms that still tread wine in lagares have added equipment that makes the work a little less tough: small destemming machines are occasionally used to separate the grapes from their stalks (if desired) and to partly crush the grapes.

Once this first tedious, hushed and sombre stage is complete, the foreman shouts *"liberdade!"*, which means freedom! Someone strikes up the music and everyone moves about freely in the lagar. In the past, the music of an accordion cheered the workers on; today, the grapes are trod to the sound of cassettes or, as I have seen for myself, to the tune of a hired musician and his electric organ, one of those that simulates all kinds of instruments.

The free-moving treading of the grapes will last another three hours as the winemaker attempts to extract the most colour through the continuous maceration of the skins. Extraction of the colour and the aromatic components that are contained in the skins is fundamental and, when the wine is made in lagares, must be done quickly as fermentation takes place more rapidly than in stainless steel vats. There is no time to lose.

The first day's lagar work ends around midnight. Fermentation will not have yet started and the must is left to rest until the next day when the treaders will return to the lagar. From now on, the wine will continue to be trod for periods of 3 hours alternating with 2 hours of rest. The rest periods are very important to the reproduction of the yeasts that, some 24 to 36 hours after the cut has ended, will trigger the start of the alcoholic fermentation.

As the must begins to ferment and the yeasts start transforming the sugar into alcohol, the appearance of the lagar changes; the work of the yeasts releases carbon dioxide that

Crushing the grapes in the lagar.

USING MEAT TO MAKE PORT?

The history of Port is full of little stories that have been handed down by mouth from father to son, some of which are legendary. Perhaps the most unbelievable one is the old wife's tale that you cannot make Port without adding meat to the wine. It may appear paradoxical, even absurd, to think that winemakers actually use meat to make their Port. The information that I obtained as I attempted to get to the roots of this tale was also given to me by mouth, as I spoke to old farmers and shippers, all of whom had retired long ago.

As you might expect, there is some basis to this story although it has been greatly embellished in its telling and one must separate the myth from the facts. The facts are that I have heard everything you could image about this matter: that you had to put a cured ham into the casks, that whole sheep were used to improve the wine and other such flights of carnivorous of fancy.

As far as I was able to determine, although I could find no written proof of this, was that cow bones, stripped of most of their meat, were used to add body to the wine; in local parlance, to "fix" the wine. One of the principle shippers actually told me that they only stopped this practice in 1970.

Yet another source informed me that bacon was used during treading. Apparently, unsalted slabs of cured bacon were placed in the lagar and were crushed by the workers along with the grapes. The yeasts in the wine would then feed off the fat that would break off from the bacon, making it easier for them to reproduce and thus trigger the fermentation. When the wine was drawn off, all the bacon had disappeared, "devoured" by the yeasts.

Another link between Port and meat is the use of dried bull's blood to fine the wine, that is, to clean it of impurities. Other winemaking regions use egg white for this purpose.

What I was never able to prove and, as far as I am concerned is pure fiction, was the use of salt ham, or presunto. I cannot see how using salted meat could in any way benefit Port.

The must, resting in the lagar, after the grapes have been crushed.

brings the skins to the surface to form a type of cap, or *manta* as it is known in the Douro. Fermentation also releases carbon dioxide and this explains why the lagares are not filled to the top. This gas is much heavier than air and it rests upon the cap to form a type of protective mantle that prevents oxygen from coming into contact with the must. The extra 25 cm form a barrier around the gas to contain it in the tank and stop it from dissipating.

The heat that is produced during fermentation rises to the surface and, if you plunge your arm in through the cap, you will note that the temperature of the must is cooler and is perfectly adequate for the fermentation to proceed correctly. The size of the lagar is also determinant as the larger the lagar, the lower the temperature at which the wine ferments.

We now enter the third stage of the lagar work; the work of extracting the most colour from the skins and the most aromatic compounds over a very short period of time. Every so often, the juice is again trod to once more macerate the skins against the rough surface of the bottom of the tank. There is clearly a greater extraction during this stage as many of the compounds are soluble in alcohol and at the higher temperatures. Treading thus continues for two or three hours, at four-hourly intervals. This work is not always done by foot inside the lagar; occasionally, men using very rudimentary tools called *macacos* – wooden staves with rows of cross sticks – stand on the edges of the lagar and push the cap down into the must from outside.

Whilst all this is being done, regular samples of must are taken and analysed to monitor the fermentation temperature, the degree of sugar (Baumé) and the density of the wine[7]. Altogether, this information will tell the winemaker exactly when he has to add the grape spirit that will arrest fermentation and transform this wine into Port.

As soon as the winemaker decides that the time has come to stop fermentation, the wine is left to rest for four hours so that all the cap can rise to the top, leaving the wine free to be drawn off through a small opening at the base of the lagar. The new wine is then transferred to a small 550-litre tank, or *lagareta*, next to the lagar. It is there that 110 litres of grape spirit are added to 440 litres of must. The brandy that is added stops fermentation as this prevents the yeasts from transforming any more sugar into alcohol; the resulting wine is naturally sweet. When a winemaker wishes to produce a dry Port, he lets the fermentation run its course until no sugars are left and only then does he add the grape spirit.

No one knows with any certainty exactly when the amount of brandy to be added to the must was set at 110 litres per pipe of wine. There is only an impression that, at the end of the 18th century, no more than 20 litres of brandy were added to each 550-litre pipe. The exact moment when the brandy is added has also varied over time, depending on whether current fashion and tastes tend more towards sweet or towards dry wines. The British have always preferred sweet, full bodied wines, as can be attested by the heated discussions that appeared in the Portuguese press during the 19th century and the many pamphlets that were published in defence of one or the other type of wine. Once the wine has been fortified in the small tank, it is then transferred to vats containing multiples of 550 litres. The pomace that remains in the lagares is then pressed, brandy is added to that juice and the resulting wine is stored in separate vats. This particular wine is very rich in aromatic components but also in tannins

---

7 Method for analysing the must to determine the alcohol potential. As fermentation develops, the Baumé degree falls. Therefore, for example, 12.5° Baumé corresponds to 11.9° of alcohol.

which is why it is often more astringent than the one that was made earlier in the lagar. It is up to the winemaker to decide whether to set it aside for blending or whether to simply add it to the wine he just made. Today, electric pumps are used to transfer the wine to vats or tanks and the dosing of the grape spirit is done by more sophisticated techniques.

The grape spirit that is used for Port today is not, contrary to what you might think, necessarily produced in the Douro. Current legislation does not even stipulate that it should be made in Portugal. Given that this is an excellent quality neutral spirit distilled from wine, with 77% alcohol by volume, its actual place of origin will not interfere with the final product. However, as the use of a less than perfect spirit could spoil an entire harvest, both producers and controlling entities have set extremely high standards for the brandy that may be used. Usually, several firms get together to purchase the brandy as a means of ensuring that it complies with these standards.

What came after the lagares?

The method of making wine in lagares still endures in the Douro, although there are many fewer working lagares today, mainly because treading grapes requires an amount of manual labour that is becoming increasingly difficult to obtain in the region. Even the most ardent supporters of treading know that, sooner or later, there will not be sufficient labour to do all the lagar work. For this reason, several firms have adopted a range of alternative solutions, one of which is the use of a mechanical robot fitted with large blades to crush the grapes. This device was designed so that when the fruit is pushed to the bottom of the lagar, the blades do not quite brush against the stone so as to avoid crushing the pips. Were the pips to be crushed, something that never happens, they would transmit unwanted rough tannins to the wine. The continuation of this myth about crushing grape pips is extraordinary. How many people have actually tried to crush a grape pip? They are so tough you would need a sledge hammer.

The robot, although a viable solution, is quite expensive which it why it will probably not come into widespread use.

Rejoicing in the lagar.

Others have made minor adjustments to the stainless steel tanks, mainly with a view to pumping wine over the cap in order to recreate, inside the tank, something similar to that which occurs in the lagar.

For some time now, all firms have stopped making their ordinary wine in lagares as the final price these fetch is far from sufficient to cover the cost of such an investment in manpower. Some firms are no longer even making their Vintage in the lagar. It was at the beginning of the '60s, after stainless steel tanks were first introduced, that Douro wineries began installing the autovinification tanks that gradually replaced the lagares.

Today, treading is usually reserved for the best grapes, those that will potentially become a Vintage. The remaining grapes are vinified in stainless steel tanks similar to those used for table wine.

MODERN WINERIES – WHERE STAINLESS STEEL TRIUMPHS

Increasingly, new wineries that are constructed in the Douro are totally equipped with stainless steel tanks for fermenting Port and for making denominated Douro table wines.

The technology that substituted the lagar method was perfected during the sixties and seventies, first with the introduction of autovinification tanks and only later, of stainless steel vats. These first experiments were somewhat discouraging as the results, in terms of quality, were far inferior to those obtained in the lagar. Twenty years had to pass before winemakers could obtain satisfactory results and before it could be shown that the new technologies could replace the lagar method without any significant loss in the quality of the final product.

Computers have become indispensable in the new wineries, with their immense number of vats for fermenting or for storing wine, as they can do much of the work that until recently was done manually. For example, computers control the entire fermentation process, thus enabling the winemaker to know, at any given moment, exactly what the situation is in each fermentation tank.

Stainless steel is, without a shadow of a doubt, the most hygienic of all materials and it reduces the possibility of attacks by bacteria to an absolute minimum. These wineries have lost all the mystique of the past and there is no trace of the folklore that is associated with the lagar. In the eyes of the visitor, a modern winery is too antiseptic and impersonal and equipped with far too much technology to make it a pole of attraction to tourists.

Modern fermentation tank.

Once the grapes arrive at the winery, several decisions have to be taken. Firstly, a sample of the juice is taken to obtain an idea of their probable alcohol content and thus, an immediate evaluation of just how ripe the grapes are. Next, depending on the grape variety, the winemaker has to decide whether he will make them into separate wines, by variety, or whether he will mix them together, and then, whether he will make a small or a large lot of wine.

The method for making of the wine in stainless steel tanks differs considerably from the lagar. As in the tanks, the winemaker can control the fermentation temperature to the last degree, fermentation in the tanks takes longer. Furthermore, he can adjust the frequency with which the juice is pumped over the cap to obtain a greater extraction of colour, another reason why fermentation in tanks usually takes longer. With this technique, which corresponds to what I earlier called the lagar work, the juice is pumped from the bottom of the tank and sprayed over the cap at the top, as often as the winemaker wants.

Adding grape spirit.

After the fermentation tanks are emptied, the must from these and the juice from the presses is piped to the storage tanks where the grape spirit is added. At this moment, the winemaker will have a first idea of the quality of the wine he has just made. He will then decide what he wants to do with it: set it aside it as a potential Vintage or LBV, reserve it for ageing in wood with a view to making a Tawny with an Indication of Age, or blend it to make a standard Ruby or Tawny.

WHICH IS THE BEST METHOD?

The answer to this question is still debated in the Douro and in Gaia. A highly emotional issue, I believe it will soon be resolved. Until the beginning of the sixties, there only was the lagar. Then, new techniques were gradually introduced to replace the lagar and, as at first they did not produce the desired results, the champions of the lagares were right in defending the traditional method.

Meanwhile, encouraged by the growing shortage of labour, technology improved and today excellent Port is made in modern wineries without resorting to lagares. In spite of these technological advances, there remains the question of why is it that the finest Vintage Ports, those that usually come out on top at blind tastings, still continue to be those that are made in lagares?

The answer to this question may lie in the great diversity of the Douro vineyards. We know that there are firms that, in addition to their own quintas, have long-standing contracts with farmers from whom they buy grapes which they use to make a Vintage with the lagar method yet their wines

Emptying a tank.

have never been able to obtain very high scores in blind tastings. In my opinion, the explanation does not reside in the fact that the wine is or is not made in a lagar, but rather that it depends on the quality of the grapes. There are small areas in the Douro that produce the most incredibly fine grapes whose quality will inevitably be transmitted to the wine whether it is made in a lagar or in a stainless steel tank. There are other areas whose grapes will never produce a first quality wine, no matter which method you use. This is the essence of the concept of the *terroir* that is so dear to the French. There are choice areas and other that will never be so. That is what is reflected in the wine.

The lagar *versus* the stainless steel tank is an issue will only be resolved when those who reserve their finest grapes for treading in a lagar start making these same best grapes wine in stainless steel tanks. The fact is, that as long as the best grapes are kept for the lagar, the lagar method will continue to make a better quality wine.

It is becoming increasingly difficult to distinguish between the product of these two methods. Wine made in the lagar has a slight taste of stems that is highly characteristic of the lagar method, and which is less apparent in a wine made in a stainless steel tank. There are, however, no major differences in terms of colour and body between either of these wines.

The twenty years that were needed to fine tune the technology developed to replace the lagares and the enormous amount of manpower they required represent a victory of science and perseverance that has placed all producers on an equal footing. Those who support the lagar method know that there are alternatives open to them. A lagar is a "hive of manpower"; a modern winery is a sterile, mechanised complex. One bears the hallmark of 300 years of history; the other sets the style for the new millennium. Fortunately, both the past and the future are still found in the Douro.

7. From the Vineyard
to the dinner table
~ the tribulations of a fortified wine

Once all the grapes have been harvested and the vintage is over, the Douro settles down to a period of apparent repose. The rogas have returned home, the hustle and bustle of the vintage is over, the lagares have been scrubbed down and the music that cheered the lagar workers is now replaced by the natural sounds of the region and by the noise of the fauna that inhabit it and attract the hunters. At the end of October, the landscape becomes completely transformed. The light mists that hung over the hills all summer, to the despair of photographers, disappear; the days are bright, the sky is clear, temperatures are mild and an refreshing tranquility reigns over all.

If you are looking for visual pleasure, this is the most beautiful time to visit the Douro. The vineyards are beginning to change colour and although some may still be covered in green leaves, others have already robed themselves in red, brown or yellow and form a kaleidoscope of rare beauty.

This calm, however, is only a mere illusion. As soon as the harvest is over, there begins a labour that requires technical expertise and the delicate touch of the artist. This is the time to examine the state of the vineyards, to correct the sulphur and brandy content of the young wines and to make sure that they are in perfect health as they will remain in the Douro over the winter and only travel to Gaia the following spring. This stay in the Douro is beneficial as the bitterly cold Douro winter helps in cleaning the wine of any floating impurities as the low temperatures cause these to precipitate to the bottom of the vats and casks, so that a first decantation has already been made by the time they are sent to Gaia.

In the old days, the wine was transported down the River Douro in the typical boats of the region, the *barcos rabelos*, that were able to transport between 30 to 70 wine casks. The journey was difficult and dangerous as the river was not navigable, in the present day sense of the word. Very narrow passages, raging rapids, slow stretches where the boats had sometimes to be pulled along the banks by oxen, there was a bit of everything – these were never routine voyages. It was only when the railway line was extended to the Douro at the end of the 19th century that the casks began to be sent down to Porto by train.

Today, the wine is sent down by road tanker, a short trip thanks to the great improvements made to the roads since the 1980s.

Not all wine is taken to Porto. One Gaia firm already transferred all its lodges to the Douro and there is the new class of producers-bottlers who keep their wines in the Douro all year round. Until 1986, only firms located in Gaia, the *shippers*, were authorised to export Port. Since then, farmers and co-operative wineries who bottle and sell their own wine can also export Port directly from the Douro. However, as the great majority of the wine is still sent to the lodges in Vila Nova de Gaia, why we can still truthfully say that Port may be created in the Douro but it is in Gaia that it ages.

Pipes of wine waiting for the train to Porto.

Why is it that the lodges are located in Gaia, across the River Douro from Porto, next to the mouth of the river? On the one hand, this was the natural consequence of wine having been shipped from there since the 17th century by sea; on the other hand, as Gaia is located on the north-facing bank of the river, the temperatures in the lodges remain pretty constant throughout the year. It is known that great temperature extremes are one of the greatest enemies of wine that is aged in wood and in this respect, Gaia has great advantages over the Douro winemaking region upriver. The high summer temperatures that assail the Douro not only speed up the ageing process as they give the wine a baked aroma, that which the trade calls the "Douro bake" and which is not easily detected by the less experienced consumer.

Once in Gaia, it is the winemaker who determines the final destination of the wine. Each firm's tasting room and laboratory is a hive of great activity in the spring. The time has come to make a first evaluation of the young wine. Samples are taken from every lot of wine made during the vintage the previous fall. This is a moment of great responsibility because it is on this evaluation that decisions will be taken as to just how the various lots will be handled. It is not rare to see a couple of hundred glasses lined up in the tasting room, corresponding to an equal number of lots of wine.

At this critical moment, the firm's "General Staff" meets so that the decisions that are taken can be consensual. Another critical and decisive moment for the firm when it debates on whether or not to declare a Vintage, but this comes later.

The standard wines are separated and set aside. Potential Vintage and LBV wines are pumped into special casks of their own, usually very large vats that help in keeping the dark purple red colour of the wine and where they are rarely disturbed, if at all, to prevent oxidation. Those that will go on to become a Tawny with an Indication of Age (10, 20, 30 and more than 40 years) or a Colheita, are pumped into small casks where they will age for the period required by law, during which they will be treated as necessary to ensure that they remain in perfect condition.

For two centuries, anything and everything that was important to Port revolved around Vila Nova de Gaia and Porto. It was here that shippers lived, where they built their offices, their lodges, their laboratories and their tasting rooms. Here, they received guests and transacted their business. This was much more a Porto than a Douro Wine.

The oenologist, as we know him today, just did not exist. What there were, were tasters, people with vast experience in the tasting room and who made up the lots. Until some thirty years ago, shippers were essentially "tasters of made wine" and not winemakers. Little or nothing was known of viticulture as a science. To speak of training vines, varieties of vine to be planted, pruning, treatments, rootstock and other aspects of viticulture was impossible for the simple reason that shippers knew next to nothing about the Douro to where they only travelled at the time of the harvest. They were much more interested in the Art of blending the wine, of which they were unqualified Masters. Making up of lots, being able to maintain a style, to understand the aromatic structure of the wines and determine their destiny was, and continues to be, an art. This art, contrary to the others, cannot be learnt just by attending a college; it is acquired over many years of practice, always under the tuition of older, more experienced tasters.

Things are different today as, far from being simple wine buyers, shippers are more and more growers and purchasers of grapes rather than of wines. The quintas are now sought after by the Gaia firms. They now receive their guests in their quintas and in the wineries that they have built, witness to an increasing interest on their part in the technical aspects of winemaking. The concept of quality begins in the vineyard and, because of that, it is increasingly evident today that one cannot remain in Gaia just making up lots; there can be no foregoing a fundamental knowledge of each vineyard, each farmer, each corner of the Douro.

An increasing number of oenologists are being employed by the sector; albeit viticulture is determinant to the quality of Port Wine, the science of winemaking, Oenology, is indispensable to producing the best quality wines.

To keep or to drink – two options

There is an old Portuguese saying that "the older wine, the better it is" and another one that is used to describe a person: "Like Port, he improves with age!".

Neither one nor the other necessarily correspond to the truth, not even when we are speaking of Port. We know that there is a great variation in the wines and the styles that are part of the great family of Port Wine. It so happens that not

Loading in Gaia.

all improve with age, which is why it is worth my saying something about this subject.

A **Port that improves with age** is one that ages well in bottle, in other words, Vintage and LBV. It is for precisely this reason that these bottles must be stored on their side, under conditions that are totally identical to those required by any other type of wine: little or no light, a temperature of between 12° and 15° C, ideally, with the minimum possible variation in temperatures and a relative humidity similar to that found in any home, that is, neither too damp or too dry. Of the LBVs, the ones that age best in bottle are those that have not been filtered, those who occasionally bear the designation of *Traditional* on the label. Other wines, those that have been pasteurised and filtered, do not improve in bottle – they don't even use the same corks as other wines, no corkscrew is needed to remove their stoppers. The latter wines must be drunk as they are purchased and these bottles should be stored in an upright position.

Ports that do not improve in bottle are standard Tawny, Ruby, Vintage Character, Tawny with an Indication of Age, Colheita and Garrafeira. This is why these are not wines that you should purchase if you expect to lay them down and hope that the wine will have improved over time. Some of these, such as Ruby, Vintage Character and the standard Tawny will actually lose their qualities if they are kept too long in bottle. You should always purchase these wines in small quantities, as you need them. When I speak of too long in bottle, I am thinking of a maximum 18 to 24 months after you buy them. You should always look at the label and purchase wines with the most recent date of bottling.

However, if you should happen to keep some Colheita type wines in your cellar, over time they may acquire some very interesting additional aromas, the so-called bottle nose, that confers them some crispness and even some elegance. Bottles of standard Tawny, Tawny with an Indication of Age, Colheita and Garrafeira Port should be stored upright. Bottles of Ruby and Vintage Character can be stored either upright or on their side.

WINING AND DINING WITH PORT

There is no such thing as the perfect way or an exact time to drink Port. Everything is allowed: drink it alone, before or after a meal or accompanied by different kinds of food, when and how you like it! Bookstores are now beginning to sell books on how to drink Port with meals and on cooking with Port. Even old regional dishes from the Douro are being brought to our attention with many suggestions as to how Port can be used, just to show that for many years the people of the region have been aware of the gastronomic virtues of Port. In spite of this being a vast subject, far too extensive to address in any detail here, I thought to include one or two or the more traditional ways to drink Port with food.

White Port continues to be an aperitif wine par excellence. In the Douro, visitors are always greeted with a glass of White Port accompanied by lightly salted Douro almonds that have been grilled in the oven or sautéed in olive oil. At the dinner table, White Port, which should always be served chilled, is also very nice with appetisers such as a *foie gras* or other paté or a fresh cheese made from cow's milk.

Vintage is traditionally drunk with cheese. The British always associate Vintage with Stilton, a very strong cheese whose taste would practically annihilate all other red wines but which goes surprisingly well with Vintage. There are two types of Portuguese cheese that go extremely well with this type of Port. On the one hand, soft goat cheeses such as the *Queijo da Serra*, in very first place, followed by *Queijo de Azeitão* and *Serpa*; on the other hand, cheeses made from cow's milk such as *Ilha* from São Jorge island in the Azores or the partly-cured *Nisa*, made from ewe's milk. However, if you are planning to serve a very old Vintage, one that is over 40 years old, I would suggest that you choose the milder of these cheeses otherwise their flavour might overpower that of the wine. Another suggestion is to serve it with an apple crumble, such as the one made from the following recipe: alternate layers of thinly-sliced tart apples, grated almonds and thin pats of butter, covered with a 1 cm-thick layer of brown sugar mixed with cinnamon, baked in the oven until done. Serve this with Vintage and you can be sure it will be a great success with your guests.

Many consumers think of **LBV** as the "poor man's Vintage" as its style is similar to that of a Vintage, it is much less expensive and goes equally well with all the above cheeses. May I suggest, however, that you be a bit daring and try a rather unorthodox association that Port lovers are beginning to delight in: *Steak au Poivre* accompanied by an LBV, preferably a young, unfiltered wine, with lots of tannins and the more rustic, the better. The fact is that the peppercorns that are lavishly spread on the meat usually overwhelm all red table wines; LBV is more than up to the task of challenging the enemy (the *steak*!).

Ruby, with its fruitiness, youth and aromas is a multipurpose wine. It can be served equally well with a wide range of cheese (except the very mildest cow's cheese), a variety of fruit such as strawberries and wild berries or red fruit desserts or pies. I would include Reserve Ruby Port in this group.

Tawny is a Port that is best drunk at the end of a meal, with a custard or a sweet, egg-based dessert. The superior quality tawnies such as a 20 Years Old or an old Colheita need no accompaniment and should be drunk at the very end of the meal. In order for you to fully enjoy all the pleasure contained in these wines, we suggest that you cool them slightly by

Vintage and Stilton: a classic association.

The flavours of Port.

placing the bottle in an ice-bucket or in the refrigerator for about twenty minutes before serving.

TO DECANT OR NOT TO DECANT

All wines may be served straight from the bottle or from a decanter. Many do not need to be decanted simply because they do not throw a deposit in the bottle although you might still prefer to transfer them to a crystal or glass decanter.

Port is no exception. Even Tawny Ports that throw no deposit in the bottle may, but do not have to be, decanted before serving. The choice is yours and depends essentially on your personal preference and on how much you wish to impress your guests.

If you decide that you are going to decant the wine, first make sure that there is no smell in the decanter. If you have a bottle of Ruby at hand, swish a little around to rinse it out and ensure that any smell of chlorine that is sometimes present in tap water is removed.

Vintage is, however, a special case and needs to be handled with care. As this wine has not been filtered, as it ages it throws a deposit in the bottle and thus it has to be decanted before serving. In addition to the question of the deposit, a

young Vintage even needs to be de-canted at least a couple of hours before service as it has to be aired so that it will release all its aromas and present the full flavour of its bouquet.

Very old Vintages and wines that are over 40 years old, should not be de-canted. In spite of their having thrown a deposit, their structure is very fragile and they may lose their aromatic qualities with the forced airing that is created by the decanting process. This is not always the case, but it is better to be safe than sorry. The best solution is to remove the bottle from your wine cellar several days before you plan to serve it (the older the wine, the longer this should be), stand the bottle upright where it won't be disturbed and serve it very, very carefully straight from the bottle. Of course, if you only decide to serve an old Vintage at the very last minute, the only solution is to carry the bottle very carefully, holding it in the same position as it had in your cellar so as not to disturb the crust and to decant it immediately afterwards.

Sometimes, but not always, the corks in very old bottles are in very poor condition and tend to crumble when you try to remove them. To ensure that this does not happen, several firms re-cork all the wines in their cellars every 25 years. However, this is not common practice. When serving an old Vintage and you are in doubt as to the condition of the cork, it is best to use hot tongs to cut the top of the bottle off at the neck, cork and all.

When you decant a Port you can either use a special funnel that is sold in speciality shops or place a clean white cotton napkin or cloth inside an ordinary funnel, to remove any floating particles or bits of cork. You should never ever use a paper filter such as the ones you find in coffee machines as they could transmit an undesirable taste to the wine. As a general rule, the older the Vintage, the more quickly it should be drunk after the bottle has been opened. Whereas a young Vintage may continue to be quite pleasant for a couple of days afterwards, an old Vintage will probably not survive more than a couple of hours in contact with the oxygen in the air.

PORT – A FOUNTAIN OF YOUTH?

Much has been written about the good and the harm that drinking Port Wine may do to your health. Some also swear that Port is responsible for the long lives of many wine lovers, particularly those who are more closely involved in the trade.

At Taylor's they tell the story of old Mr. Yeatman who, when he was well advanced in years, went to London for his annual check-up. As his usual physician was away, he was examined by a young doctor who, amazed with his remarkable good health, decided to ask him some further questions regarding his living habits.

"Do you drink any wine, Mr. Yeatman?"

"Yes."

"What wine do you drink?"

"Port, of course."

"How much Port do you drink?"

"Not much. About a pipe a year..."

A pipe! That is about 720 bottles! Now, with an average of 6 glasses per bottle, that is 12 glasses a day. And that, as any true devotee in the trade will tell you, is not really farfetched ...

The temperature at which Vintage should be served should be similar to the one in the cellar where it was stored. If served too cold, its tannins will be accentuated; if served too warm it will lose a lot of its bouquet and it is the alcohol in the wine that will come out.

GLASSES AND CEREMONY

The ideal glasses are tulip-shaped, similar to those internationally approved by the O.I.V. There are several manufacturers and models, but I personally recommend the Reidel glasses. This Austrian firm offers two types of Port glasses: one for Vintage and one for Tawny. Although they are apparently very similar their respective purposes are very different. Ideally, one should buy both types of glasses; if you carry out a comparative tasting of the two models, you will see that Vintage is clearly impaired when drunk from the Tawny glass and vice versa. Of course, if you can't have both, either model will do very well for both types of Port.

There is ceremony to serving Port and everyone is endeavouring to ensure that it does not fall into disuse. When you serve your guests a Vintage, the decanter is placed before the host who first tastes it to make sure it is fit to drink. The host then serves the guest on his right and then passes the decanter to the guest on his left who then passes it on to his left, and so on, always clockwise. As traditions are to be maintained, a simple phrase such as: "Excuse me, is your passport in order?" is usually sufficient to draw the attention of a guest who has served himself and forgotten to pass the decanter on.

Another favourite custom is to ask your guests to guess the age of the Vintage and, if possible, the name of the shipper. It is not unusual for a Vintage to show much younger than the guests think it is and it is not so easy to name the shipper as the different house styles are not that easily detected.

It is becoming increasingly customary to associate cigars with Port, particularly Vintage. The traditional association Cognac-Cigar is thus changing and today there are more and more cigar aficionados (including myself) who prefer to accompany a "Cuban delight" with a Vintage Port. This trend is extremely fashionable but it does require a bit of common sense. The fact is that the smell of the cigar will fill the room and create an atmosphere in which it becomes almost impossible to enjoy the full bouquet of a Vintage. This is why it is recommended that cigars are only lit after the Vintage has already gone around the table once and everyone present, especially the non-smokers, has had a chance to appreciate the magnificent aroma that fills the room when you open a bottle of Port.

VINTAGE – WHICH SHOULD YOU BUY?

When you buy a Vintage you must first consider what you intend to do with it – do you plan to lay it down in your wine cellar or are you going to serve it in the near future? If what you intend is to invest in a Vintage and lay it down to age, I recommend that you look out for young Vintages when they are first offered to the market. At that time they will be less expensive, there will have been less speculation, the market is well supplied with the wine and they are easier to obtain. When you buy a Vintage for laying down, you should store the bottles on their side in the same conditions of temperature, light and humidity that you would obey for any other type of red wine.

If you are looking for a Vintage to serve immediately, I would recommend 1970 (expensive), 1977 (expensive), 1978 (good price), 1983 (good price), 1984 (good price). If, on the other hand, you are looking for a wine to lay down, I would recommend 80, 85, 87, 91, 94 and 95. Keep a special eye out for the excellent 97 Vintage that has just been declared. You may drink some now but be sure to keep some cases for future occasions.

8. The Institutions

*T*he institutional structure of the Port sector has undergone many changes throughout its history. Under Salazar's *Estado Novo*, the government created a corporate model based on three pillars: a Port Shippers Guild; an official controlling entity – the Port Wine Institute; and a Farmers Federation – the Casa do Douro.

This model lasted until 1974 when it was changed following the revolution of the 25th of April. It was then that farmers began to challenge the monopoly that shippers held over exports and shippers began to challenge the vast powers of the Casa do Douro.

There was a considerable amount of unrest in the Douro and in Gaia in the years that immediately followed the revolution, proof that many of the wounds created by decades (not to say, centuries) of animosity between farmers and merchants, were far from healed. It was only in the 80s and 90s that the first major structural changes were to be made to the sector.

In response to a more than deserving aspiration of farmers, Port was now allowed to be shipped from the Douro which meant that farmers were no longer dependent on the firms in Gaia. The first Douro producers-bottlers of Port were established in 1986. In spite of the fact that the amount of Port they made and shipped was very limited, the principle of the freedom to export had been established, thus putting an end to a dependence that made no sense.

Another significant step in changing the institutional structure of the sector was the creation of the Interprofessional Committee for the Douro Demarcated Region (CIRDD) in 1995. This committee, formed by farmers and merchants and one representative of the government, has assumed many of the responsibilities that used to belong exclusively to the Casa do Douro. The entire Port Denomination of Origin is now in the hands of the CIRDD, the core entity for the sector. Soon, it will also be responsible for all the other denominations of origin in the region (DOC Douro, Regional Wine, Moscatel and Espumante).

The **Port Wine Institute** (*Instituto do Vinho do Porto* – IVP), whose Board of Governors is appointed by the government, is responsible for certifying, supervising and promoting the Port Denomination of Origin. Certification is essentially the duty of its Panel of Tasters who approve the wines and the grape spirit and the granting of the Guarantee Seal. Supervision of the trade is based on the of Current Stock Account that the IVP maintains for each firm. These records are constantly updated and not a drop can be marketed without first checking the stock account. No operator in the sector can market a wine that has not been previously declared to the IVP (no matter how long ago) as a wine of a given category or one that is not listed in the IVP records.

In the case of the grape spirit, the IVP also maintains up-to-date records for each operator. The IVP cross-checks the amount of brandy a farmer/operator was entitled to under the benefício he was allocated against the amount of spirit that he actually used during the vintage.

The IVP inspectors may make on-site visits to firms to verify their stock and take samples of any lot of wine for analysis for purposes of comparing the amounts declared by the firm and its actual current stock account. In the event of a full company audit, the inspectors go through the entire stock with a fine-tooth comb, examining and taking samples of every single cask. This type of inspection, one that brings to mind the days of Prohibition, tends to occur less often than in the past although it is still carried out in cases where fraud is suspected or, more frequently today, when the IVP is asked by a firm to stand as guarantor for a loan against the firm's stock of wine.

Now that the CIRDD is operating in the Douro, all the wine is checked in the Douro before it is transported to Gaia in sealed containers; when it arrives in Gaia, all the documents are again checked and the seals are examined to ensure they have not been tampered with. Today, much of the inspection is done on the basis of daily spot-checks and the end of the production chain (that is, during bottling) where the wine that is being bottled can be checked against the IVP's records (don't forget that Port is no longer sold in bulk).

It is the IVP that is responsible, following an agreement within the framework of the CIRDD, for determining the amount of must each year for which benefício can be apportioned. This so-called Vintage Manifesto, is published before the beginning of the harvest. Based on the amount that is published, a farmer can determine how much must from his vineyards will obtain a benefício card and, consequently, the amount of grape spirit that he will be permitted to purchase to fortify this wine and make it into Port.

The **Casa do Douro** is the entity that represents the farmers; as all farmers are required, by law, to register with it, it is responsible for the upkeep and updating of this list. For the moment, all payments to farmers from firms are still made through the Casa do Douro. Therefore, whenever a firm contracts with a farmer to purchase his grapes, payment must be by cheque handed over to the Casa do Douro who will send it on to the farmer. The vineyard register continues to be filed with the Casa do Douro although it is soon to be transferred to the CIRDD.

The Casa do Douro also represents the 23 Co-operative Wineries of the region; it is also responsible for certifying the DOC Douro wines.

With an extraordinarily large stock that it built up over the years by purchasing surplus wine from farmers, the Casa do Douro got involved in some very questionable business when it attempted to buy 40% of the share capital in Real Companhia Velha, the only large Port firm that does not belong to the AEVP. With the failure of the deal, the Casa do Douro ended up being dependent on grants and subsidies from the government, sums that, as one well knows, only postpone but do not solve financial problems.

The **Association of Port Wine Companies** (AEVP – *Associação das Empresas de Vinho do Porto*) began its existence as the Port Shippers Guild and in 1975, changed its name to Association of Port Shippers. Its name has again been altered to reflect that now that the Gaia shippers no longer have the monopoly over exports, it is an association of all firms, including small producers. Altogether, this Association represents the overwhelming majority of those involved in the Port trade.

The AEVP has a seat on the Interprofessional Committee, on a par with the farmers who are represented there by the Casa do Douro. Its duties include the defence and promotion of the Denomination of Origin and representing its members at international meetings and all other events in which the trade should be present.

The AEVP co-ordinates all the activities of the Visitor Centres at the Gaia lodges, with a view to standardising the manner by which visitors are received and to guarantee a quality service to the many thousands of tourists who visit Gaia each year.

AVEPOD – *Associação dos Viticultores Engarrafadores dos Vinhos do Porto e Douro* is the Association that represents all the producers-bottlers who are not members of the AEVP. It does not have a seat on any of the official institutions with responsibilities in the Douro.

Unidouro represents the 23 co-operative wineries in the region and which produce 60% of all the table wine and 40% of all the Port made in the Douro. Altogether, it represents something like 10,000 farmers and 20,000 hectares of vineyards.

acidity
essential element in wine. Contributes to a feeling of freshness in the mouth. Indispensable to the longevity of the wine and to its harmony. Too little acidity makes a wine that is insipid, listless and lacking in spirit. Too much acidity and you get a caustic and acid taste in the mouth.

alcohol
essential element in wine. Results from the transformation, by yeasts, of the sugar in the must during fermentation.

alcoholic fermentation
the process by which the yeasts in wine transform sugar into alcohol.

Americano
Portuguese name for the wine made from Concord grapes grown on hybrid rootstock that was not grafted with *vitis vinifera.*

astringent
used to describe a wine that creates a sharp, acid feeling inside the mouth. Results from too many tannins and is normally accompanied by a high acidity. Usually noted in young wine and in wine made from grapes that are still attached to their stems. Tends to diminish with age in bottle.

austere
said of a wine that does not "show" itself, that remains closed, that needs time to develop.

balseiro
Portuguese name for the large, cone-shaped vats that are used for storing large quantities of Port.

blind tasting
a method for tasting wine by which the taster does not know which wine he is tasting as the bottle or bottles have been covered up. Common practice when tasting several wines from a same region made by different producers.

body
the "fullness" of a wine in the mouth as a result of its alcohol content and the dry extract it contains.

bouquet
set of complex aromas present in great wines. A superior quality wine requires several years to develop its bouquet.

bright
an essential characteristic of a wine, particularly white wine; obtained by decanting and filtering. Red wine that has not been filtered may throw a deposit in bottle and thus require the utmost care when it is served.

bulk
wine sold in cask, not in bottle, without a Guarantee Seal.

cap
thick layer of grape skins that have floated to the top of the must once fermentation has begun. The cap has to be repeatedly pushed down or pumped over with must to extract the most amount of colour from the skins.

cask
generic term for wooden wine containers, i.e., pipe.

colouring matter
elements in grape skins that give wine its colour.

crisp
said of a wine that has a high acidity, especially white wine. A desirable characteristic.

curtimenta
Portuguese name for the wine-making technique by which the must is fermented on the grape skins.

D.O.C.
Controlled Denomination of Origin, from the old French expression for Demarcated Region: *Dénomination d'Origine Controllée.*

decanting
expression with two meanings: in winemaking, this is one of the techniques with white wine to separate the must from the skins after it has macerated; for the consumer, this is the process by which a wine is carefully poured from the bottle into a decanter to enable a wine to breathe; recommended for red wines and absolutely essential for some Port that throw a deposit in bottle, such as Vintage and traditional LBV.

destemming
operation that consists of separating the grapes from their stalks. Wine that is fermented in contact with the stems (traditional method) may have an unpleasant, vegetal aroma.

drawing off
process of removing wine that has just been made, from a tank. An opening at the bottom of the treading tank is unplugged and the wine is allowed to run out clear, leaving the pomace behind.

dry extract
solid particles in wine (except sugars); a light wine has little dry extract; a full-bodied wine has a lot.

dry wine
a wine that has no, or negligible amounts of, residual sugars.

filtration
cleansing of wine before it is bottled with a view to removing all floating particles. Indispensable with white wine. Not essential with red wine, except perhaps ordinary wine. A wine that has been excessively filtered is said to have been scraped.

finesse
from the French. Synonymous with delicacy and sensitive flavours; even a highly structured wine may have finesse if all its elements are well balanced.

finish
the sensation left in the mouth by a wine. A great wine always has a long finish. A short, dry finish is synonymous with a high amount of volatile acids.

fortified wine
wine to which brandy was added during fermentation to stop all its sugars from being transformed into alcohol. This wine is sweeter and has a higher alcohol content than table wine. In Portugal, the finest fortified wines are Port, Madeira and Moscatel.

fruity
said of a wine that has aromas of fruit (primary aromas), the result of a winemaking that has respected the characteristics of the variety of grapes from which it was made.

grafting
to attach a vine or part of a vine (the scion) to an established plant (the rootstock) which supports and nourishes it. This operation became compulsory after the phylloxera.

harmony
feeling of equilibrium between the various elements in a wine: alcohol, acidity and tannins; well balanced.

hectare
land measure corresponding to 10,000 square metres or 2,471 acres.

iodine
aroma present in very old fortified wine.

L.B.V.
standard abbreviation for Late Bottled Vintage Port.

lagar
Portuguese name for the granite treading tank.

Late Bottled Vintage
special category of Port: a superior quality wine, deep purple in colour, made in a single year and bottled between the 4th and 6th year after the grapes were harvested. The label must indicate the year in which it was made.

light
said of a wine that has little body.

lot
a blend of wines of different origins and ages. Tawny Port is a blended wine.

macaco
Portuguese name for a rudimentary wooden instrument used in the treading tanks to push the cap down into the must.

maceration of the skins
winemaking technique used for white wine that consists in keeping the grape skins in contact with the juice in order to extract the most aroma before they are removed prior to fermentation The expression is not used for red wine as usually the skins usually are left in the must during fermentation.

malolactic fermentation
the process by which the lactic bacteria transform malic acid into lactic acid. This may occur during alcoholic fermentation or afterwards. In the event this is not controlled it may result in a secondary fermentation in bottle that creates a gas and makes a wine unpleasant.

maturation
period during which the grapes ripen, usually about 45 days. At this time the acidity decreases as the sugar content of the grapes rises.

metallic
an undesirable aroma, likened to that of fountain pen ink, that is often noted in wine and results when the tannins in the wine come into contact with iron or copper.

must
the juice that is obtained by crushing grapes. Becomes wine after fermentation.

oenology
the science of winemaking and all that it involves.

oidium
disease that strikes the vine in the spring and requires preventive treatment. It was in an attempt to combat an epidemic of oidium during the 19th century that the American vines were introduced to Europe, unbeknownst that these were infested with the phylloxera.

oily
said of an impression that a wine may leave in the mouth; expression associated with wines from hot climates that are made with overripe grapes; may also be synonymous with buttery.

organoleptic tasting
sensory appreciation of wine
– colour, aroma and taste.
The same expression is applied
to other food products such
as olive oil.

oxidation
changes to a wine through contact with oxygen. Unwanted in
young table wine, may occur
with old wine due to bad corks
or poor storage. In some cases
such as aged Port, oxidation is
indispensable as this confers
characteristic aromas.

past it
said of an oxidised table wine or
one that no longer has any posi-
tive organoleptic characteristics.

phylloxera
a microscopic insect, or nematode, that attacks and destroys
the roots of grapevines. Came to
in Europe during the 19th century from America. It is still present in the soil, which is why
European vines continue to be
grafted onto rootstock that is
immune to its effects.

pipe
a wine cask. In the Port trade, a
shipping pipe contains 550 litres
(the standard measure used for
apportioning licences); lodge
pipes, used to store wine in Gaia,
are often larger (between 580
and 630 litres). The value of a
quinta is measured by the number of pipes of Port it is licenced
to make (benefício).

poor
said of a wine that lacks structure – little body, few tannins,
short on the finish.

precipitation
the sinking, through gravity, of
solid matter that is floating in
the wine.

press wine
wine made from the juice
obtained from pressing the
pumice that remains in the tank
when the new wine has been
drawn off. Usually very tannic
and should only be used for
blending.

pomace
the solid matter – skins, stems,
stalks, and pips – that are left in
a tank once the new wine has
been drawn off.

Quinta
Portuguese word for wine estate.
In the Douro, essentially used to
describe a vineyard as a quinta
does not necessarily have any
buildings on it.

residual sugars
sugars contained in the must
that are not transformed into
alcohol during fermentation.
Apparent in sweet wines. The
winemaker may choose to halt
fermentation at a certain point
in order to create a wine with
a high sugar content. This is
what occurs with Port and other
fortified wine where brandy is
added to stop fermentation.
With other types of wines, the
same effect is obtained by
adding sulphurous acid.

root stock
a vine that will be planted directly into the soil and onto which a
selected variety of grapevine
will be grafted. Used since the
end of the 19th century as it is
resistant to the phylloxera.

rot
affectation of the grape resulting
from the effects of a fungus that
grows in bad weather conditions
such as rain during maturation.

rounded

said of a wine that is well balanced, warm, all enveloping.

Ruby

a young Port Wine whose name is taken from the precious stone of the same colour.

scraped

said of a wine that has been filtered too much and left with little or no body.

skins

enclosing the grapes, these contain important elements such as colorants, tannins and aromas.

spirit

made from distilling wine or brandy. Only grape spirit is permitted for Port.

structure

internal organisation of a wine. Good structure is obtained from good grapes and good winemaking practice. Structure involves the body, alcohol, tannins and complexity of a wine.

sulphurous acid

used in wine as an antiseptic, anti-oxidant and preserving agent. Inhibits the formation of microorganisms that might be harmful to wine and encourages longevity. A wine to which sulphurous acid has not been added usually becomes a hothouse for germs.

tank

large deposit used for fermenting must or for storing wine. Preferably made of stainless steel although there are some specially lined cement tanks.

tannin

essential element in wine that comes from the skins and from young wood. Indispensable to the longevity of wine, may create a sharp taste in the mouth when a wine is too young when it is drunk.

tartaric acid

the principal acid in wine that gives it the health it needs to live. In the cases of a wine that is low in acids, it is recommended that tartaric acid be added as this will improve the overall quality of the wine.

tartrates

tartaric acid crystals that form in cold temperatures. May form on the bottom of bottles of wine that has not been cold-treated. Not a negative factor.

Tawny

golden reddish brown. Most common type of Port whose colour is acquired through long periods of ageing in cask and through oxidation. Port with an Indication of Age (10, 20, 30, 40 and More than 40 Years Old) also belongs to this category; must be approved by the Port Wine Institute.

temperature control

consists of keeping the temperature at which a wine is fermenting between certain limits in order to extract most of the aromas in the grapes. Essential to both white and red wine. There are several methods for doing this.

treading tank

tank built of blocks of granite where the grapes are crushed by foot and where the fermentation of the must occurs. Treading tanks vary in size but usually have a capacity measured as multiples of 550 litres (capacity of a pipe).

trimming

a form of pruning of the vine that is carried out when the

bunches of grapes are beginning
to form (June); by removing a
certain number of bunches in
each vine, one attempts to
increase the concentration and
the quality of those that are left
to develop.

unctuous
said of a smooth, full wine with
a high glycerine content.

varietal
a variety of grapevine. One of
the principal elements that char-
acterises a wine and gives it its
typical nature. The same varietal
planted in different soils and
weather conditions produces different types of wine, although
some of the aromatic elements
that are typical of the varietal
will remain the same.

vat
an extremely large wood cask.

velvety
very soft in the mouth.
Apparent in fortified wine and in
some superior quality, old table
wine.

vertical tasting
tasting of several wines that all
have a common factor: these
may be wines from different
years from a same producer,
wines from a same year from different regions or, wines from a
same variety of vine from different regions.

Vinho Fino
Old Portuguese word for Port
Wine. Still used with pride by
some Douro farmers when referring to their very own superior
quality wine.

Vintage
special category of Port Wine,
corresponding to the top of the
range. Deep purple red wine, of
superior quality, from a single

year and bottled between the
2nd and the 3rd year after the
grapes have been harvested. As
opposed to Tawny, Vintage ages
in bottle. Must be approved by
the Port Wine Institute.

viticulture
the science that studies the set
of operations necessary to creating, planting and caring for a
vineyard and the vines.

vitis vinifera
generic scientific name for the
class of European grapevines;
other types of vines that do not
pertain to this class are considered hybrid vines and are known
in Portugal as American vines.

volatile acids
elements present in wine that,
when excessive, create a vine-
gary aroma. Too much is the
result of poor care during winemaking. Older wines may have a
touch more volatile acidity. The
Portuguese call this *vinagrinho*; it
is highly appreciated.

winemaking
the Art that involves the set of
operations necessary to transform grapes into wine.

winery
place where all the work involved in transforming grapes into
wine is done.

yeasts
microscopic organisms that, during fermentation, turn the sugars
in the grapes into alcohol.
Present in the grape skins
and, when insufficient, may be
added to the juice to enable
fermentation.

Attachments

AEVP – Association of Port Wine Companies. List of members.

A. A. CÁLEM & FILHO, SA.
Av. Diogo Leite, 25/42
4400-111 Vila Nova de Gaia
Apartado n° 140
4401 Vila Nova de Gaia Codex
Gaia – Tel.: 223746660 Fax: 223746699
Web Site: http://www.calem.pt
E-mail: calem@calem.pt

A. A. FERREIRA, SA
Rua da Carvalhosa, 19/103
4400-082 Vila Nova de Gaia
Tel.: 223745292
Fax: 23759732
Centro de Visitas – Tel.: 223746100

ADRIANO RAMOS-PINTO – VINHOS, SA
Av. de Ramos-Pinto, 380
4400-266 Vila Nova de Gaia
Apartado n° 1320
4401 Vila Nova de Gaia Codex
Tel.: 223707000
Fax: 223793121
E-mail: rp.vinhos@mail.telepac.pt

BARROS, ALMEIDA & CA. -VINHOS, SA
Rua D.Leonor de Freitas, 180/2
4400-123 Vila Nova de Gaia
Apartado n° 39
4431 Vila Nova de Gaia
Tel.: 223752320/ 223752420/ 223752445
Fax: 223751939
Web Site: http://www.porto-barros.pt
E-mail: info@porto-barros.pt

C D VINTNERS, SOCIEDADE VITIVINÍCOLA, SA.
Largo de Joaquim Magalhães, 23
4400-187 Vila Nova de Gaia
Apartado n° 1318
4401 Vila Nova de Gaia Codex
Tel.: 223772950
Fax: 223707166

C.N. KOPKE & CA. – VINHOS, SA
Rua de Serpa Pinto, 183/191
4400-307 Vila Nova de Gaia
Apartado n° 42
4401 Vila Nova de Gaia Codex
Tel.: 223752320/223752420/223752445
Web Site: http://www.porto-barros.pt
E-mail: info@porto-barros.pt

C. DA SILVA (VINHOS), SA
Rua de Felizardo Lima, 247
4400-140 Vila Nova de Gaia
Apartado n° 1530
4401 Vila Nova de Gaia Codex
Tel.: 223746040
Fax: 223746049
E-mail: c.dasilva@mail.telepac.pt

CASTELINHO, VINHOS, SA.
Quinta de S. Domingos
Apartado 140
5050 Peso da Régua
Tel.: 254/320100
Fax: 254/320109

CHURCHILL GRAHAM, LDA.
Rua da Fonte Nova, 5
4400-156 Vila Nova de Gaia
Tel.: 223703641 Fax: 223703642
Web Site: http://www.churchill's-port.com
E-mail: churchill.s@mail.telepac.pt

COCKBURN SMITHES & CA., SA.
Rua das Coradas, 13
4400-099 Vila Nova de Gaia
Apartado n° 20
4401 Vila Nova de Gaia Codex
Tel.: 223776500
Fax: 223776599
E-mail: antonio-graca@adsweu.com

FONSECA GUIMARAENS – VINHOS, SA
Rua Rei Ramiro, 316
4400-283 Vila Nova de Gaia
Tel.: 223719999
Fax: 223795570 (Administrativo/
/Financeiro) – 223707321 (Administração)
223708607 (Marketing)
Web Site: http://www.fonseca.pt
E-mail: marketing@fonseca.pt

FORRESTER & CA., SA.
Rua Guilherme Braga, 38
4400-174 Vila Nova de Gaia
Apartado n° 1309
4401 Vila Nova de Gaia Codex
Tel.: 223746060
Fax: 223793805

**GRAN CRUZ PORTO – SOCIEDADE
COMERCIAL DE VINHOS, LDA.**
Rua José Mariani, 390
4400-195 Vila Nova de Gaia
Tel.: 223702222/356/355
Fax: 223700033

HUNT CONSTANTINO-VINHOS, SA
Rua da Carvalhosa, 19/103
4400-082 Vila Nova de Gaia
Tel.: 223745292
Fax: 223759732

J. CARVALHO MACEDO, LDA.
Av. de Ramos-Pinto, 400
4400-266 Vila Nova de Gaia
Apartado n° 1320
4401 Vila Nova de Gaia Codex
Tel.: 223707700
E-mail: rp.vinhos@mail.telepac.pt

J.H. ANDRESEN, SUCRS., LDA.
Rua de Felizardo de Lima, 74
4400-140 Vila Nova de Gaia
Apartado n° 1510
4401 Vila Nova de Gaia Codex
Tel.: 223770450 Fax: 223770458
E-mail: jha@mail.telepac.pt

J.W. BURMESTER & CA., SA
Rua de Belmonte, 39
4050-097 Porto
Tel.: 223321274/223321299/222056977
Fax: 222054331
E-mail: burma@mail.telepac.pt

MANOEL D. POÇAS JUNIOR – VINHOS, SA
Rua Visconde das Devesas, 186
4400-337 Vila Nova de Gaia Codex
Apartado n° 1556
4401 Vila Nova de Gaia Codex
Tel.: 223771070
Fax: 223771079
Web Site: http://www.portugaloffer.co-
m/pocas_vinhos/index.html
E-mail: export@pocas.pt

MARTINEZ GASSIOT & CO., LTD.
Rua das Coradas, 13
4400-099 Vila Nova de Gaia
Apartado n° 20
4401 Vila Nova de Gaia Codex
Tel.: 223776500
Fax: 223776599
E-mail: antonio-graca@adsweu.com

NIEPOORT (VINHOS), SA
Rua do Infante D. Henrique, 16 -2°
4050-296 Porto
Apartado 6003
4051 Porto Codex
Tel.: 222080473/222080660–223751640
(armazém Gaia)
Fax: 223320209
E-mail: niepoort@mail.telepac.pt

**OSBORNE PORTUGAL – VINHOS,
DISTRIBUIÇÃO E SERVIÇOS, LDA**
Rua Cândido dos Reis, 670
4400-071 Vila Nova de Gaia
Tel.: 223752648/223794842
Fax: 223757517
E-mail: oportugal@osborne.es

**PRODUTORES ASSOCIADOS DE VINHOS
PROGRESSO DO DOURO, LDA.**
Rua da Lousada – Godim
5050 Peso da Régua
Tel.: 254/320358
Fax: 254/320368
E-mail: caves.vale@mail.telepac.pt

QUARLES HARRIS & CA., LDA.
Rua do Barão de Forrester, 12
4400-034 Vila Nova de Gaia
Apartado nº 26
4401 Vila Nova de Gaia Codex
Tel.: 223776300
Web Site: http://www.symington.com
E-mail: symington@symington.com

QUINTA DO NOVAL – VINHOS, SA
Av. Diogo Leite, 256
4400-111 Vila Nova de Gaia
Apartado nº 1319
4401 Vila nova de Gaia Codex
Tel.: 223752020/223752045/223798414
Fax: 223750365
Centro de Visitas: 223770282
Web Site: http://www.quintadonoval.pt
E-mail: novalport@mail.telepac.pt

ROMARIZ – VINHOS, SA.
Rua Rei Ramiro, 316
4400-281 Vila Nova de Gaia
Apartado nº 1312
4401-501 Vila Nova de Gaia Codex
Tel.: 223756980
Fax: 223706725
E-mail: romariz@romariz.pt

ROZÈS, SA
Rua Cândido dos Reis, 526/532
4400-070 Vila Nova de Gaia
Apartado nº 376
4401 Vila Nova de Gaia Codex
Tel.: 223771680
Fax: 223771689
Web Site: http://www.rozesport.com
E-mail: marketing@rozesport.com

**S. PEDRO DAS AGUIAS – SOC. AGR.
COMERCIAL, SA**
Lugar dos Enxudos – 5120 Tabuaço
Tel.: 254/781464
Fax: 254/781014
E-mail: porto.s.pedro@mail.telepac.pt

SANDEMAN & CA., SA
Largo de Miguel Bombarda, 3
4400-222 Vila Nova de Gaia
Apartado nº 1308
4401 Vila Nova de Gaia Codex
Tel.: 223740500
Fax: 223706816
Web Site: http://www.sandeman.com
E-mail: the_don@sandeman.com

SILVA & COSENS, LTD.
Boavista – Travessa Barão de Forrester
4400-034 Vila Nova de Gaia
Apartado nº 14
4401 Vila Nova de Gaia Codex
Tel.: 223776300
Fax: 223776301
Web Site: http://www.dows-port.com
E-mail: dowsport@dows-port.com

SMITH WOODHOUSE & CA., LDA.
Rua Rei Ramiro, 514
4400-281 Vila Nova de Gaia
Apartado nº 26
4401 Vila Nova de Gaia Codex
Tel.: 223776300
Fax: 223776301
Web Site:
http://www.smithwoodhouse.com
E-mail: symington@symington.com

**SOCIEDADE AGRICOLA E COMERCIAL
DOS VINHOS MESSIAS, SA**
Rua de Felizardo de Lima, 140/8
4400-140 Vila Nova de Gaia
Apartado nº 1566
4401 Vila Nova de Gaia Codex
Apartado nº 1 – 3050 Mealhada Codex
Gaia – Tel.: 223745770
Fax: 223745779
Mealhada – Tel.: 231/202027/8
Fax: 231/202026
E-mail: caves.messias@mail.telepac.pt

SOCIEDADE QUINTA DO PORTAL, SA
Rua Guilhermina Suggia, 200 – 9º
4200-318 Porto
Apartado 52057
4202-801 Porto
Tel.: 225512000
Fax: 225512099
Web site: http://www.quintadoportal.com
E-mail: quintaportal@mail.telepac.pt

SOCIEDADE DOS VINHOS BORGES, SA
Rua General Torres, 923
4400-164 Vila Nova de Gaia
Apartado nº 27
4401 Vila Nova de Gaia Codex
Tel.: 223755002/223755027/223755471
Fax: 223754985

SOLAR DA REDE - SOCIEDADE DE EXPLORAÇÃO TURÍSTICA E AGRÍCOLA; LDA.
Rede - Santa Cristina
5040 Mesão Frio
Tel.: 254890130
Fax.: 254890139
Rua de S. Francisco, 4 - 2º Dtº
4050-548 Porto
Tel.: 223393950
Fax: 222083407

TAYLOR, FLADGATE & YEATMAN – VINHOS, SA
Rua do Choupelo, 250
4400-088 Vila Nova de Gaia
Apartado nº 1311
4401 Vila Nova de Gaia Codex
Tel.: 223719999/223793430
Fax: 223795570 (Financ/Adm.)
223700949 (Vendas/Produção)
223707321 (Administração)
Web Site: http://www.taylor.pt
E-mail: marketing@taylor.pt

W. & J. GRAHAM & CO.
Quinta do Agro – Rua Rei Ramiro, 514
4400-281 Vila Nova de Gaia
Apartado nº 19
4401 Vila Nova de Gaia Codex
Tel.: 223776300
Fax: 223776301
Web Site: http://www.grahams-port.com
E-mail: grahams@grahams.com

WARRE & CA., SA
Travessa do Barão de Forrester, 85
4400-034 Vila Nova de Gaia
Apartado nº 26 – 4401 Vila Nova de Gaia
Tel.: 223776300 (30 linhas)
Fax: 223776301
Web Site: http://www.warre.com
E-mail: warre@warre.com

WIESE & KROHN, SUCRS., LDA.
Rua Dr. António Granjo, 122
4400-124 Vila Nova de Gaia
Apartado nº 1
4401 Vila Nova de Gaia Codex
Tel.: 223751238/223752216
Fax: 223771729
E-mail: Krohn@mail.telepac.pt

Other addresses

AEVP – ASSOCIAÇÃO DAS EMPRESAS DE VINHO DO PORTO
Rua Barão de Forrester, 412
4400-034 Vila Nova de Gaia
Tel.: 351 22 374 55 20
Fax: 351 22 370 54 00
E-mail: aevp@mail.telepac.pt
Web site: http:www.aevp.pt

CIRRD – COMISSÃO INTERPROFISSIONAL DA REGIÃO DEMARCADA DO DOURO
Rua dos Camilos - Edifício Casa do Douro
5050 - 272 Peso da Régua
Tel.: 351 254 320 850
Fax: 351 254 320 899
E-mail: cirrd@mail.telepac.pt
Web site: http://www.cirrd.pt

IVP – INSTITUTO DO VINHO DO PORTO
Rua de Ferreira Borges
4050-253 Porto
Tel.: 351 22 207 16 00
Fax: 351 22 207 16 99
E-mail: ivp@ivp.pt
Web site: http://www.ivp.pt

CASA DO DOURO
Rua dos Camilos
5050 - 272 Peso da Régua
Tel.: 351 254 320 811
Fax: 351 254 320 800
E-mail: casadodouro@mail.telepac.pt

GABINETE DA ROTA DO VINHO DO PORTO
Rua dos Camilos, 90
5050 - 272 Peso da Régua
Tel.: 351 254 320 145
Fax: 351 254 320 149
Web site: http://www.ivp.pt